Water–Energy–Food–Ecosystem–Climate Nexus: Advancing Climate Resilience, Sustainable Development, Resource Efficiency, Renewable Energy, Ecosystem Protection, and Food Security

I0029947

1

Copyright

Water–Energy–Food–Ecosystem–Climate Nexus: Advancing Climate Resilience, Sustainable Development, Resource Efficiency, Renewable Energy, Ecosystem Protection, and Food Security

© 2025 Robert C. Brears

All rights reserved.

No part of this publication may be reproduced, stored in a retrieval system, or transmitted in any form or by any means—electronic, mechanical, photocopying, recording, or otherwise—without the prior written permission of the publisher, except in the case of brief quotations used in reviews, articles, or academic analysis.

The author and publisher are of the same opinion regarding the views and content expressed in this work.

Disclaimer: The information in this book is provided for general knowledge and educational purposes only. While every effort has been made to ensure accuracy, the author and publisher make no representations or warranties with respect to the completeness or suitability of the content. The author and publisher accept no liability for any errors, omissions, or outcomes resulting from the application of information contained herein. Readers are advised to consult appropriate professionals or authorities before acting on any material presented.

ISBN (eBook): 978-1-991368-43-0

ISBN (Paperback): 978-1-991368-44-7

Published by Global Climate Solutions

First Edition, 2025

Cover design and interior layout by Global Climate Solutions

Table of Contents

Introduction

The interconnected systems of water, energy, food, ecosystems, and climate shape the foundation of global sustainability. Each system influences and depends on the others, forming a complex web that determines environmental stability and human well-being. As populations grow and resource demands intensify, managing these interdependencies becomes increasingly critical to ensure resilience and equity across regions and generations.

The Water–Energy–Food–Ecosystem–Climate (WEFEC) Nexus provides a holistic framework for understanding and addressing these interconnections. It emphasizes the need for integrated approaches that move beyond single-sector management to consider how actions in one area affect others. Through this lens, resource efficiency, governance, and sustainability are pursued simultaneously, recognizing that water security cannot be achieved without sustainable energy, that food production depends on both water and energy, and that healthy ecosystems underpin the stability of all three while influencing and being influenced by climate dynamics.

Adopting a Nexus perspective allows decision-makers to identify co-benefits and trade-offs among sectors. For instance, renewable energy projects can reduce emissions but may compete with agriculture for land and water. Conversely, sustainable agricultural practices can enhance carbon sequestration while reducing water use. These examples demonstrate how policies, technologies, and investments must be aligned to achieve multiple objectives across the WEFEC framework rather than optimizing one at the expense of others.

Climate change serves as a unifying driver that amplifies pressures within the Nexus. Shifts in temperature, precipitation, and extreme weather patterns directly affect water availability, agricultural yields, and energy supply. The degradation of ecosystems further undermines natural resilience, reducing the capacity to adapt to these changing conditions. Integrated management approaches that link climate adaptation, resource conservation, and sustainable development are essential to address such challenges comprehensively.

Governance plays a central role in operationalizing the Nexus. Institutional collaboration across ministries, sectors, and administrative levels is required to bridge policy gaps and coordinate resource management. Equally important are financial mechanisms and data-driven tools that support cross-sectoral planning, enabling governments and organizations to make informed decisions under uncertainty. Innovation, including digital technologies and nature-based solutions, strengthens this coordination by providing insights into resource flows and ecosystem services.

The WEFEC Nexus is not a theoretical construct but a practical approach to achieving sustainability goals. It aligns with international commitments such as the Sustainable Development Goals, the Paris Agreement, and biodiversity frameworks, which all emphasize the importance of integrated action. By fostering cooperation among governments, industries, and communities, the Nexus perspective enables the transition toward efficient, equitable, and climate-resilient systems that balance economic growth with environmental integrity.

This book explores the WEFEC Nexus through interconnected themes covering governance, technology, resource systems, and financing. It provides analytical insights into how integration can enhance sustainability across sectors and scales. The chapters that follow examine each component of the Nexus and the mechanisms that enable their alignment, offering pathways toward coordinated solutions for a rapidly changing world.

Chapter 1: Understanding the WEFEC Nexus

The WEFEC Nexus represents a systems-based approach to managing interconnected resources that sustain life and economic activity. It recognizes that actions in one domain—such as water use or energy production—inevitably influence others, creating both challenges and opportunities for sustainable development. By linking resource flows, ecosystem functions, and climate dynamics, the Nexus framework promotes integrated planning and policy coherence. Understanding these interdependencies enables decision-makers to design strategies that enhance efficiency, reduce trade-offs, and build resilience in the face of growing resource demand, environmental degradation, and climate variability.

Conceptual Foundations

The WEFEC Nexus provides a systems-based approach to understanding how interconnected natural and human systems influence each other. It highlights that managing one sector independently often leads to inefficiencies or unintended consequences in others. By viewing these systems as interdependent, the Nexus approach seeks to balance resource security, environmental sustainability, and human well-being through coordinated management and integrated policy design.

At the core of the Nexus is the principle of interconnectivity. Water, energy, food, ecosystems, and climate are linked through physical flows, economic exchanges, and ecological functions. Water supports energy production and agriculture; energy powers water treatment and food supply chains; ecosystems provide the services necessary to sustain both water and food systems; and all are affected by and contribute to changes in the climate. Recognizing these interdependencies allows for more effective resource allocation and avoids the risks associated with fragmented decision-making.

The conceptual foundation of the WEFEC Nexus rests on the understanding that human activities depend on the continuous exchange of resources within ecological boundaries. Natural systems regulate resource flows, while human systems determine how those resources are used. This relationship is dynamic and shaped by demographic growth, technological development, and policy choices. The Nexus framework provides a structured method for identifying critical connections and leverage points where interventions can achieve multiple outcomes simultaneously. It supports the transition from linear, resource-intensive systems toward more circular and regenerative models.

Resource scarcity and competition are central concerns within the Nexus. Population growth, urbanization, and industrial expansion increase demand for water, energy, and food while placing pressure on ecosystems that provide essential services. Without coordinated management, these demands can lead to overexploitation, degradation, and conflict. The Nexus perspective encourages policies that promote efficiency and resilience, reducing vulnerability to resource shocks and climate variability. Integrating Nexus principles into planning ensures that environmental limits are respected and long-term sustainability is maintained.

Governance structures play an essential role in operationalizing the Nexus concept. Traditional sectoral governance—where water, energy, agriculture, and environment are managed separately—limits the ability to coordinate across interlinked systems. Institutional reforms that promote cross-sectoral collaboration, shared data systems, and integrated monitoring can align decision-making processes with Nexus objectives. Effective governance also requires the participation of multiple stakeholders, including local communities, private enterprises, and international organizations, to ensure inclusive and equitable outcomes.

The Nexus framework also depends on the application of science and technology to understand and manage complex interdependencies. Advances in data analytics, remote sensing, and modeling provide new insights into resource flows and environmental feedbacks. These tools enable the assessment of trade-offs, support evidence-based policymaking, and guide adaptive management. Digitalization and real-time monitoring enhance transparency, helping decision-makers respond quickly to emerging challenges.

Social and economic dimensions are integral to the Nexus. Equity, access, and distributional fairness must be considered alongside efficiency and sustainability. Vulnerable populations often bear the greatest burden of resource scarcity and environmental degradation. Incorporating social considerations into Nexus-based strategies ensures that interventions address inequality while enhancing overall system resilience. This inclusive approach aligns with global sustainability goals and supports a just transition toward climate-resilient development.

The WEFEC Nexus serves as a conceptual bridge between scientific understanding and practical implementation. It emphasizes that achieving sustainability requires viewing human and natural systems as interconnected rather than separate domains. By fostering integration across sectors and scales, the Nexus framework helps societies anticipate challenges, manage trade-offs, and pursue policies that sustain resources for future generations.

Historical Evolution of Nexus Thinking

The origins of Nexus thinking can be traced to the early concepts of integrated resource management that emerged in the mid-twentieth century. As nations began to industrialize rapidly, resource consumption grew exponentially, leading to increasing pressure on natural systems. Early environmental policies primarily addressed single sectors—such as water supply or agricultural production—without accounting for cross-sectoral impacts. Over time, it became evident that such compartmentalized approaches failed to address the interconnected nature of environmental and socio-economic challenges. The realization that resources were interdependent laid the foundation for more comprehensive management frameworks.

The 1970s marked a turning point with the global recognition of environmental limits. The oil crises of 1973 and 1979 highlighted the vulnerability of energy systems, while severe droughts and famines underscored the fragility of water and food systems. The 1972 United Nations Conference on the Human Environment in Stockholm emphasized the need for integrated planning to balance economic development with environmental protection. This decade witnessed the growing understanding that water, energy, and food security were intertwined, even though formal Nexus terminology had not yet been introduced. These developments led to the adoption of early integrated approaches, particularly in water resource management.

In the following decades, integrated water resources management (IWRM) became the dominant framework for linking environmental, social, and economic objectives. Initiated in the 1980s and formalized at the 1992 Dublin Conference on Water and the Environment, IWRM called for coordinated development and management of water, land, and related resources. While effective in some contexts, IWRM remained largely focused on the water sector, often overlooking systemic interactions with energy production, food systems, and climate dynamics. This limitation later prompted the expansion of thinking toward broader resource interconnections.

By the early 2000s, growing evidence of climate change and resource competition renewed global attention on systemic integration. The Millennium Ecosystem Assessment (2005) and the Intergovernmental Panel on Climate Change (IPCC) reports highlighted the interdependence of ecosystem health, resource availability, and human well-being. At the same time, economic globalization intensified resource flows and dependencies between regions, making sectoral management increasingly inadequate. The need for a multidimensional framework that could guide decision-making across water, energy, and food systems became widely recognized.

The concept of the Water–Energy–Food Nexus gained formal recognition in international policy dialogues following the 2011

Bonn Conference on "The Water, Energy and Food Security Nexus." Organized by Germany's Federal Government, this event framed the Nexus as a strategic approach to achieving sustainable development through integrated policy design. The conference linked the Nexus directly to the global sustainability agenda, emphasizing efficiency, equity, and environmental protection as guiding principles. Subsequent summits and research initiatives built on this foundation, extending the framework to include ecosystem services and climate systems, giving rise to the modern WEFEC Nexus.

The inclusion of ecosystems and climate within the Nexus framework reflected a growing understanding that natural systems are not passive resources but active regulators of water, energy, and food security. This expanded scope aligned the Nexus with the Sustainable Development Goals (SDGs), particularly those addressing water (SDG 6), energy (SDG 7), food (SDG 2), and climate action (SDG 13). The approach has since been adopted by international organizations, national governments, and research institutions seeking to operationalize integrated resource management. The evolution of Nexus thinking thus represents a progression from sectoral management to a systemic paradigm that recognizes the interconnected nature of human and environmental systems.

Key Interconnections and Feedback Loops

The WEFEC Nexus is defined by the intricate interactions and feedback mechanisms that link natural and human systems. Each element influences the others through biophysical and socioeconomic processes, creating complex dependencies that determine sustainability outcomes. Recognizing these interconnections is essential for identifying opportunities to optimize resource efficiency and minimize trade-offs between sectors.

Water, energy, and food form the foundation of human survival and economic development, while ecosystems and climate regulate the conditions under which these resources exist. Energy production requires water for extraction, processing, and cooling; water systems depend on energy for pumping, treatment, and distribution; and food systems depend on both water and energy for cultivation, processing, and transport. This cyclical dependence means that stress or inefficiency in one area reverberates across others. For example, droughts can limit hydropower generation and irrigation potential, increasing reliance on fossil fuels and affecting food availability.

Feedback loops within the Nexus operate through both natural and human-driven processes. Positive feedbacks can amplify changes, while negative feedbacks can stabilize systems. Climate change intensifies positive feedback loops by increasing temperatures that drive higher water demand and energy consumption. Conversely, ecosystem restoration can create negative feedbacks that mitigate environmental stress, such as through carbon sequestration or enhanced water retention in landscapes. Understanding the direction and strength of these feedbacks helps identify leverage points for sustainable interventions.

Ecosystems play a pivotal role in regulating feedbacks between water, energy, and food systems. Forests, wetlands, and soils act as natural buffers, storing water, regulating flows, and maintaining carbon balance. When these ecosystems degrade, feedback loops often shift toward instability, increasing vulnerability to floods, droughts, and temperature extremes. Healthy ecosystems thus serve as stabilizing agents in the Nexus, enhancing resilience across all interconnected systems. Conversely, their degradation can trigger cascading failures, such as declining agricultural productivity and reduced water quality.

Economic and policy systems introduce additional feedback mechanisms that influence how resources are managed. Price signals, subsidies, and regulatory frameworks can either reinforce sustainable behaviors or exacerbate resource stress. For instance, energy subsidies that lower fuel costs can lead to excessive groundwater extraction for irrigation, which depletes aquifers and disrupts ecosystem services. Conversely, pricing reforms that reflect environmental costs can realign incentives, encouraging efficiency and conservation. These human-centered feedbacks highlight the role of governance in shaping the outcomes of Nexus interactions.

Technological change also modifies feedback relationships across the Nexus. Innovations such as renewable energy, precision irrigation, and wastewater recycling alter traditional dependencies by reducing resource intensity and diversifying supply sources. However, new technologies can create unintended feedbacks if deployed without integrated planning. Large-scale bioenergy production, for example, can compete with food crops for land and water, while desalination plants can increase energy demand and emissions if powered by fossil fuels. Anticipating these consequences requires system-wide analysis rather than sector-specific assessments.

Social and institutional factors further influence feedback dynamics through patterns of behavior, consumption, and governance. Population growth and urbanization intensify demand across all resource systems, while changes in dietary preferences or energy use can shift feedback loops in unexpected ways. Institutional coordination—or lack thereof—determines how effectively societies can manage these evolving pressures. Cross-sectoral communication and integrated data systems are essential for detecting feedback signals early and adjusting policies accordingly.

Climate change acts as both a driver and an amplifier within the WEFEC Nexus. Altered precipitation patterns affect water availability, influencing food production and energy generation. Rising temperatures increase energy demand for cooling, while changing weather patterns disrupt agricultural yields. These shifts feed back into global markets and governance systems, influencing investment, trade, and adaptation strategies. The integration of climate considerations into resource planning ensures that feedback mechanisms are understood and managed proactively.

The interaction between natural and human feedback loops defines the stability of the WEFEC Nexus. When feedbacks are balanced, systems can adapt and maintain functionality under stress. When feedbacks are reinforcing or misaligned, small disruptions can escalate into crises. Managing these interconnections requires continuous monitoring, flexible governance, and adaptive strategies that account for uncertainty and change. Understanding feedback dynamics provides the foundation for anticipating challenges and designing resilient, interconnected systems that sustain both human and ecological well-being.

Global Relevance and Policy Integration

The WEFEC Nexus has become an essential framework in global policy and sustainable development discourse. Its significance lies in promoting integrated solutions that address interconnected challenges rather than sector-specific goals. The Nexus approach aligns with global sustainability objectives by emphasizing efficiency, equity, and resilience across resource systems. As resource demand intensifies and environmental degradation accelerates, coordinated policy frameworks are increasingly necessary to ensure sustainable outcomes at national and international levels.

The SDGs reflect the integrated logic of the Nexus. Adopted in 2015 by the United Nations, the SDGs aim to end poverty, protect the planet, and promote prosperity through 17 interlinked goals. Nexus thinking directly supports the implementation of multiple goals, particularly those related to clean water and sanitation (SDG 6), affordable and clean energy (SDG 7), zero hunger (SDG 2), climate action (SDG 13), and life on land (SDG 15). Achieving one goal often depends on progress in others—for example, energy access supports irrigation, which improves food security, while sustainable land and water management strengthen ecosystem services and climate resilience. This interconnectedness requires policies that transcend traditional sectoral boundaries.

Global climate governance frameworks, such as the Paris Agreement, incorporate Nexus principles through the integration of adaptation and mitigation strategies. The Agreement recognizes that achieving emission reduction targets depends on transforming energy systems, enhancing land use practices, and protecting ecosystems. Nexus-based approaches can help countries meet their nationally determined contributions (NDCs) by promoting resource efficiency and low-carbon development. Integrating water and energy planning, for example, reduces the carbon intensity of water systems and enhances resilience to climate variability. The alignment of Nexus thinking with climate policy supports both immediate environmental goals and long-term economic stability.

The Convention on Biological Diversity (CBD) further reinforces the role of ecosystems within the Nexus framework. Biodiversity conservation underpins the provision of ecosystem services essential to water regulation, food production, and climate moderation. The CBD's post-2020 Global Biodiversity Framework calls for mainstreaming biodiversity across all sectors, reflecting the same integrated principles that guide the WEFEC Nexus. Coordinated efforts between environmental and resource management institutions ensure that economic activities contribute to the preservation of natural systems that sustain life and development.

International organizations such as the Food and Agriculture Organization (FAO), the United Nations Environment Programme (UNEP), and the United Nations Framework Convention on Climate Change (UNFCCC) have adopted Nexus-based methodologies to guide national policy integration. These organizations provide technical guidance and capacity-building programs to help countries design strategies that link water, energy, food, and ecosystems within climate adaptation and mitigation agendas. Regional initiatives—such as those within the European Union, the African Union, and the Association of Southeast Asian Nations—demonstrate how multilateral cooperation can operationalize Nexus principles through shared governance and resource management mechanisms.

Policy integration within the Nexus framework also depends on coherence among national strategies. Governments are increasingly adopting cross-sectoral approaches that harmonize water, energy, agriculture, and environment ministries. This coordination reduces policy fragmentation, prevents conflicting objectives, and maximizes the effectiveness of resource use. Tools such as integrated resource planning, environmental-economic accounting, and system modeling support evidence-based decision-making, allowing policymakers to assess trade-offs and identify co-benefits across sectors. Institutional mechanisms, including inter-ministerial councils and multi-stakeholder platforms, strengthen collaboration and ensure that policies remain aligned with sustainable development objectives.

Financing and investment frameworks play a crucial role in translating global commitments into action. International funds, including the Green Climate Fund (GCF) and the Global Environment Facility (GEF), prioritize projects that demonstrate cross-sectoral benefits consistent with Nexus principles. These mechanisms encourage countries to design projects that deliver climate resilience, energy efficiency, and ecosystem restoration simultaneously. Aligning financial flows with Nexus objectives helps bridge the gap between high-level policy commitments and tangible on-the-ground outcomes.

Data integration and knowledge sharing further enhance the implementation of the Nexus approach at global and national scales. Open data platforms, collaborative research networks, and shared monitoring systems enable policymakers and practitioners to access and apply scientific evidence. This exchange of information supports the harmonization of methodologies and strengthens accountability in achieving sustainability targets. International collaboration on data collection and modeling ensures that decisions are informed by comprehensive, transparent, and up-to-date evidence.

The WEFEC Nexus underpins a growing movement toward integrated sustainability governance. It provides a framework for linking global commitments with local actions and for reconciling environmental protection with socio-economic development. By aligning policies, institutions, and financial mechanisms under a unified approach, the Nexus enables more coherent, effective, and equitable pathways toward global sustainability.

Chapter 2: Water as the Central Nexus Component

Water lies at the core of the WEFEC Nexus, underpinning all natural and human systems. It is essential for energy production, agricultural productivity, ecosystem stability, and climate regulation. As pressures from population growth, economic expansion, and climate change intensify, managing water resources sustainably becomes increasingly complex. The interconnections between water and other sectors highlight the need for integrated governance and efficient allocation to ensure long-term resource security. Understanding water's central role in the Nexus framework provides a foundation for aligning policies, technologies, and investments that balance competing demands while preserving ecological integrity.

Water's Role in Energy and Food Systems

Water plays a central role in sustaining both energy production and food systems, linking these two essential sectors through complex physical, economic, and environmental interdependencies. The reliability of water resources determines the stability of energy supply and agricultural productivity, while demands from these sectors in turn affect water availability and quality. Understanding and managing these connections is critical to ensure balanced resource allocation, minimize competition, and maintain long-term sustainability across all sectors.

In the energy sector, water is indispensable for multiple stages of production, conversion, and distribution. Thermal power plants, which include coal, natural gas, and nuclear facilities, rely heavily on water for cooling processes to maintain safe and efficient operations. Hydropower generation, while renewable and non-emitting, depends entirely on sufficient water flows and reservoir storage, making it highly sensitive to climatic variability and hydrological changes. Additionally, water is required in the extraction and processing of fossil fuels, such as in shale gas operations, which use water for hydraulic fracturing, and in oil refining, where it is necessary for cleaning, heating, and chemical treatment. These demands position water as a critical input in virtually all conventional and renewable energy systems.

The emergence of renewable energy technologies has shifted, but not eliminated, water's importance in the energy landscape. While solar photovoltaics and wind power require minimal water during operation, concentrated solar power (CSP) and bioenergy production still depend significantly on water resources. Bioenergy crops, in particular, introduce competition for land and water with food systems, especially in regions already facing scarcity. This competition can increase vulnerability to droughts and disrupt agricultural supply chains. Efficient irrigation, wastewater reuse, and technological innovation in cooling systems—such as dry and hybrid cooling—are essential for reducing the water footprint of energy systems and enhancing their resilience under changing climatic conditions.

Water also underpins food systems through its critical role in agricultural production, livestock management, and food processing. Irrigation supports crop yields in regions with limited or irregular rainfall, yet it accounts for approximately 70 percent of global freshwater withdrawals. The type of irrigation system, crop selection, and local climatic conditions all determine water demand intensity. Traditional flood irrigation remains prevalent in many regions but is inefficient compared to modern systems such as drip or sprinkler irrigation, which deliver water directly to plant roots and minimize losses through evaporation and runoff. The adoption of these technologies can substantially improve efficiency and reduce pressure on shared water resources, though their widespread implementation often depends on financial and institutional capacity.

The interdependence of water, energy, and food creates complex feedback mechanisms that influence both production and consumption patterns. Energy is needed to pump, transport, and treat water for agricultural use, while agricultural practices affect the energy required for water management. For example, intensive irrigation increases energy demand for groundwater pumping, particularly where aquifers are deep or overexploited. Similarly, energy-intensive desalination technologies are becoming increasingly important in arid regions to ensure reliable irrigation supplies. These dynamics demonstrate how water management decisions have cascading implications for energy consumption, emissions, and economic costs across sectors.

Climate change further intensifies the interconnection between water, energy, and food systems. Rising temperatures and shifting precipitation patterns alter water availability, affecting hydropower potential, thermal plant efficiency, and crop yields. Prolonged droughts and increased evaporation rates reduce surface and groundwater storage, heightening competition between agricultural and energy users. Conversely, extreme rainfall events and floods can disrupt infrastructure, damage crops, and contaminate water sources. Integrated adaptation measures—such as diversified energy portfolios, improved irrigation efficiency, and the use of treated wastewater in agriculture—help buffer these risks while maintaining productivity.

Governance plays a crucial role in managing the interdependencies of water, energy, and food systems. Fragmented sectoral policies often lead to inefficiencies and conflict over resource allocation. Effective governance frameworks promote coordination between ministries and stakeholders, aligning water resource management with energy and agricultural planning. Mechanisms such as integrated water–energy–food assessments and cross-sectoral policy platforms enable informed decision-making based on system-wide impacts rather than isolated objectives. Regulatory measures, pricing reforms, and incentives for efficient technology adoption can reinforce sustainable practices across sectors.

Technological advancement is increasingly important in optimizing water use within energy and food systems. Precision agriculture leverages sensors and remote monitoring to optimize irrigation timing and volume, reducing waste and improving yields. In the energy sector, innovations in wastewater reuse and closed-loop cooling systems are reducing freshwater withdrawals. Digital tools, including satellite-based monitoring and predictive analytics, enhance the capacity to manage water resources dynamically across competing demands.

The centrality of water to both energy production and food systems underscores its role as the connecting element within the broader WEFEC Nexus. Managing these interdependencies requires not only technological and infrastructural improvements but also institutional collaboration, data integration, and policy coherence. As pressures on water resources intensify, the capacity to balance its competing uses across sectors will determine the sustainability and resilience of societies in the face of accelerating environmental and economic change.

Aquatic Ecosystems and Climate Regulation

Aquatic ecosystems, including rivers, lakes, wetlands, estuaries, and oceans, are fundamental to global environmental stability. They regulate climate by storing and cycling carbon, controlling energy flows, and supporting nutrient and hydrological processes essential to life. These systems form a bridge between terrestrial and atmospheric environments, influencing temperature regulation, precipitation patterns, and food productivity. Their ecological integrity determines the resilience of the broader WEFEC Nexus.

Aquatic ecosystems act as vital carbon sinks. Oceans absorb a significant share of atmospheric carbon dioxide through physical and biological processes, including photosynthesis by phytoplankton and the sequestration of organic material in marine sediments. Inland water bodies, such as wetlands and peatlands, store vast amounts of carbon in biomass and soil. When these systems are degraded through pollution, drainage, or overexploitation, stored carbon is released back into the atmosphere, exacerbating climate change. Maintaining the health of aquatic systems is therefore integral to achieving climate mitigation targets and stabilizing global carbon balances.

Water quality and nutrient cycling are closely tied to the ecological function of aquatic systems. Nutrients such as nitrogen and phosphorus are recycled through complex food webs involving aquatic plants, microorganisms, and animals. Balanced nutrient cycles support biodiversity and primary productivity, while nutrient imbalances from agricultural runoff or wastewater discharge can cause eutrophication. Excess nutrients lead to algal blooms that deplete oxygen, reduce biodiversity, and emit greenhouse gases such as methane and nitrous oxide. The management of nutrient inputs is a critical element of maintaining ecosystem health and preventing climate-relevant feedbacks.

Wetlands serve as one of the most effective natural infrastructures for regulating climate and hydrology. They absorb floodwaters, recharge groundwater, and filter pollutants, maintaining both water quality and regional climate stability. Through evapotranspiration, wetlands moderate local temperatures and contribute to atmospheric moisture regulation. Despite their importance, many wetlands have been lost to urbanization, agriculture, and industrial expansion, diminishing their capacity to provide ecosystem services. Protecting and restoring these areas is an essential component of sustainable resource management within the Nexus framework.

Aquatic ecosystems also influence food and energy systems through their role in supporting fisheries, irrigation, and hydropower. Rivers and lakes provide freshwater for agriculture and energy generation, while coastal ecosystems sustain global fisheries that supply a major portion of the world's protein. These functions depend on the ecological balance of aquatic environments, which can be disrupted by overfishing, sedimentation, and pollution. Energy and agricultural practices that alter water flows or introduce contaminants can degrade ecosystem functions, leading to cascading effects across multiple sectors. Ensuring that human use remains within ecological limits is essential for preserving both productivity and resilience.

Climate change is reshaping aquatic ecosystems through warming waters, altered precipitation, and rising sea levels. Higher temperatures reduce dissolved oxygen levels, stressing aquatic organisms and altering species distribution. Shifts in rainfall patterns influence river discharge and groundwater recharge, while melting glaciers and ice caps change sediment dynamics and nutrient delivery to downstream ecosystems. In coastal areas, sea-level rise increases salinity intrusion into freshwater systems, affecting both ecosystems and human water supplies. These climate-driven changes highlight the need for adaptive management that integrates ecosystem health into broader water and climate policies.

Governance and management approaches that value ecosystem services can help align environmental and economic objectives. Integrating aquatic ecosystem conservation into water, energy, and food planning ensures that ecological functions are recognized as critical components of sustainable development. Policy instruments such as environmental flow requirements, pollution controls, and protected area designations safeguard ecosystem processes. Economic valuation of ecosystem services provides further incentive for conservation by highlighting their contributions to livelihoods, water regulation, and climate mitigation.

Aquatic ecosystems form the foundation of planetary resilience by linking hydrological, biological, and climatic systems. Their capacity to regulate carbon and nutrient cycles, support biodiversity, and stabilize regional climates underscores their central role within the WEFEC Nexus. Sustaining their integrity requires integrated management approaches that recognize their multiple contributions to environmental balance, human well-being, and long-term climate stability.

Governance and Institutional Integration

Integrated Water Resources Management (IWRM) has long served as a guiding framework for addressing the complex interactions between water use, environmental sustainability, and socio-economic development. Its primary goal is to balance competing demands for water among various sectors—agriculture, industry, energy, and ecosystems—while ensuring equitable access and long-term resource security. Within the broader WEFEC Nexus, IWRM offers a foundational governance model that promotes coordination and shared responsibility. However, institutional fragmentation, overlapping mandates, and limited intersectoral communication remain persistent barriers to realizing the full potential of Nexus integration.

Governance within the WEFEC Nexus involves coordinating multiple actors operating at different administrative scales. Water management authorities, agricultural ministries, energy regulators, and environmental agencies often function independently, guided by distinct objectives and regulatory frameworks. This compartmentalized approach hinders the ability to manage interconnections effectively. For example, agricultural expansion policies may not account for water scarcity implications, or energy development plans may overlook impacts on aquatic ecosystems. Institutional integration requires a shift toward holistic planning processes that align goals, harmonize regulations, and create mechanisms for joint decision-making.

Institutional coherence begins with the development of shared policy frameworks that explicitly recognize cross-sectoral dependencies. Governments can establish inter-ministerial committees or councils tasked with aligning water, energy, food, and environmental policies. Such bodies facilitate dialogue among agencies and help avoid duplication or contradiction in policy implementation. Formal coordination mechanisms can be reinforced through legislation that mandates collaborative planning and integrated monitoring. Internationally, transboundary cooperation mechanisms, such as river basin organizations, illustrate how joint governance structures can address shared resource challenges effectively.

Legal and regulatory instruments play a critical role in embedding Nexus principles into governance systems. Laws governing water rights, energy production, land use, and pollution control often operate independently, creating inefficiencies and conflicts. Revising these frameworks to include cross-sectoral provisions helps ensure that decisions in one sector consider their broader implications. For instance, energy licensing procedures can incorporate environmental flow requirements, or agricultural subsidy schemes can include incentives for water efficiency and soil conservation. Regulatory coherence supports accountability and reduces unintended trade-offs between sectors.

Institutional capacity building is essential to bridge the gap between conceptual integration and practical implementation. Training programs, joint research initiatives, and data-sharing platforms enhance understanding of interdependencies across ministries and agencies. Cross-sectoral technical expertise enables policymakers to evaluate the systemic effects of decisions, while integrated data management systems provide the evidence base needed for informed planning. Strengthening local governance capacity is equally important, as local authorities often play a key role in implementing policies related to water, land, and resource management.

Stakeholder engagement forms another critical dimension of effective governance. The WEFEC Nexus encompasses a wide range of actors, including government institutions, private enterprises, civil society, and local communities. Inclusive participation ensures that diverse perspectives and needs are incorporated into decision-making, enhancing legitimacy and effectiveness. Public–private partnerships can mobilize investment and innovation, while community-led initiatives promote adaptive management and social equity. Transparent communication channels and participatory processes foster trust and facilitate the negotiation of trade-offs among competing interests.

Decentralization is another governance strategy that can enhance integration when carefully managed. Delegating responsibilities to regional or local authorities allows for context-specific management of resources and the incorporation of traditional knowledge into decision-making. However, decentralization must be accompanied by adequate funding, technical support, and oversight to prevent inconsistencies and ensure alignment with national strategies. Balancing centralized coordination with local autonomy creates a governance structure that combines strategic coherence with flexibility.

Adaptive governance is increasingly recognized as a necessary approach within the WEFEC Nexus. Given the uncertainties associated with climate change and socio-economic transformation, static policy frameworks are insufficient. Adaptive governance emphasizes learning, flexibility, and iterative decision-making based on monitoring outcomes and adjusting strategies as conditions evolve. This approach allows institutions to respond to emerging challenges, incorporate new knowledge, and continuously improve policy effectiveness.

Institutional integration under the Nexus framework requires political commitment and long-term vision. Successful implementation depends on sustained leadership, inter-agency coordination, and resource allocation to support integrated planning and monitoring. The process involves transforming governance systems from reactive management toward proactive collaboration across sectors. By embedding Nexus thinking into legal frameworks, institutional structures, and administrative practices, governments can enhance efficiency, equity, and resilience in managing interconnected resource systems.

Water Security under Climate Stress

Climate change exerts a profound influence on the availability, quality, and distribution of freshwater resources. Rising global temperatures intensify the hydrological cycle, altering precipitation patterns, evaporation rates, and runoff dynamics. These shifts affect both surface and groundwater systems, heightening the risk of scarcity in some regions while increasing flooding in others. Water security, defined as the reliable availability of sufficient water to sustain livelihoods, health, ecosystems, and economic growth, is increasingly challenged by these climatic pressures. Managing water resources under climate stress requires integrated and adaptive strategies that address both short-term variability and long-term change.

Changes in precipitation regimes are among the most visible effects of climate stress on water systems. Many regions experience intensified rainfall events leading to floods, while others suffer prolonged droughts that deplete reservoirs and aquifers. The uneven distribution of precipitation disrupts established water management systems, particularly in areas reliant on predictable seasonal patterns. Diminished snowpacks and glacial retreat in high-altitude regions reduce natural storage, affecting river flow and downstream availability during dry seasons. These shifts compromise irrigation systems, hydropower production, and municipal water supplies, demanding improved forecasting, storage infrastructure, and policy coordination.

Runoff variability further complicates the management of freshwater resources. In many basins, increasing temperatures accelerate evaporation, reducing available water even in regions with stable precipitation. Higher evapotranspiration rates amplify soil moisture loss, affecting both natural vegetation and agricultural productivity. In contrast, extreme rainfall can lead to flash floods that erode topsoil, damage infrastructure, and contaminate drinking water sources with sediment and pollutants. The dual challenge of scarcity and excess requires adaptive planning that integrates water storage, flood control, and watershed management.

Groundwater systems, which act as buffers against climate variability, face growing stress from over-extraction and reduced recharge. In arid and semi-arid regions, dependence on aquifers has increased as surface supplies become unreliable. However, declining recharge rates due to altered precipitation and land-use changes threaten the sustainability of these reserves. Overexploitation leads to falling water tables, land subsidence, and degradation of water quality through salinization and contamination. Sustainable groundwater management must include improved monitoring, regulation of withdrawals, and promotion of recharge-enhancing practices such as managed aquifer replenishment and restoration of infiltration zones.

Water quality degradation is an additional dimension of climate-induced stress. Rising temperatures accelerate algal growth in lakes and reservoirs, increasing treatment costs and reducing water suitability for consumption. Flood events transport agricultural chemicals, pathogens, and waste into waterways, while droughts concentrate pollutants by reducing dilution capacity. These impacts undermine ecosystem health and human well-being. Integrating water quality management into climate adaptation strategies is critical to maintaining safe and resilient water systems. Investments in wastewater treatment, pollution prevention, and nature-based filtration systems can enhance water security in a changing climate.

Adaptive water management under climate stress emphasizes flexibility, learning, and collaboration across sectors. Traditional planning approaches, which rely on historical climate data, are no longer sufficient in an era of rapid change. Instead, adaptive management incorporates scenario planning, iterative decision-making, and the continuous adjustment of strategies based on observed outcomes. This approach supports resilience by allowing institutions to respond dynamically to shifting conditions. Implementing adaptive measures requires robust data systems, predictive modeling, and effective governance that facilitates coordination between water, energy, agriculture, and environmental agencies.

Resilience planning complements adaptation by strengthening the capacity of systems and communities to absorb and recover from climate-related shocks. It involves diversifying water sources, improving storage efficiency, and promoting water-saving technologies across sectors. Infrastructure design increasingly integrates flexibility to withstand a range of climate extremes, from drought-resistant supply systems to flood-resilient urban drainage. Social and institutional resilience is equally important, involving education, stakeholder participation, and community-based management to foster collective responsibility and preparedness.

Efficiency improvements are central to achieving water security under climate stress. Reducing losses in distribution networks, adopting water-efficient technologies in agriculture and industry, and promoting behavioral changes in consumption can substantially alleviate pressure on water systems. Efficiency also extends to energy and food systems that depend on water inputs, creating opportunities for cross-sectoral gains. For example, optimizing irrigation reduces both water use and energy demand for pumping, while reusing treated wastewater supports agricultural production without depleting freshwater resources.

Ensuring long-term water security in the face of climate change demands integrated governance that unites environmental, economic, and social objectives. Policies must link climate adaptation with resource management, ensuring that water allocation decisions support both human and ecosystem needs. Strengthening institutions, investing in resilient infrastructure, and incorporating scientific knowledge into planning are key to sustaining water resources under increasing climatic uncertainty. By embedding adaptive, efficient, and inclusive strategies within governance systems, societies can safeguard water security amid a changing global climate.

Chapter 3: Energy in the Nexus Framework

Energy is the driving force behind the interconnected systems of water, food, ecosystems, and climate. It powers water treatment and distribution, supports agricultural production, and influences emissions that affect climate stability. As economies expand and populations grow, global energy demand continues to rise, creating mounting pressures on natural resources and infrastructure. Within the WEFEC Nexus, energy acts as both an enabler of development and a source of vulnerability when mismanaged. Understanding energy's role within this framework is essential for identifying pathways toward cleaner production, efficiency gains, and integrated resource governance that align with sustainability goals.

Energy Demand across Nexus Sectors

Energy serves as a fundamental driver across all components of the WEFEC Nexus. It enables the treatment, transport, and distribution of water; powers agricultural production and food processing; supports ecosystem management; and underpins infrastructure critical for climate adaptation and mitigation. The flow of energy through these interconnected systems reveals both opportunities for efficiency and vulnerabilities to disruption. Understanding cross-sectoral energy demand is essential for ensuring sustainable resource management and enhancing resilience to environmental and economic pressures.

Water systems depend heavily on energy for their operation. Extraction from surface and groundwater sources, desalination, pumping, treatment, and distribution all require significant power inputs. In many urban regions, the energy intensity of water systems is rising due to deeper groundwater withdrawals, expansion of desalination capacity, and the need for advanced treatment to maintain water quality. Wastewater treatment facilities are also energy-intensive, particularly those using advanced nutrient removal or water recycling technologies. However, opportunities exist to improve efficiency and recover energy from these systems, such as through biogas generation, improved process control, and integration with renewable power sources.

Agriculture is one of the largest consumers of both water and energy. Energy powers irrigation pumps, greenhouses, fertilizer production, food processing, and cold chain logistics. In irrigated agriculture, energy demand depends on pumping depth, water availability, and the efficiency of distribution systems. In regions reliant on fossil fuel–powered irrigation, energy use contributes significantly to emissions and operating costs. Transitioning to renewable energy–based irrigation and efficient technologies, such as drip systems, can reduce both energy consumption and water withdrawals. Similarly, fertilizer and pesticide production accounts for a substantial share of agricultural energy use. The adoption of organic and regenerative farming practices can mitigate energy inputs while maintaining productivity.

The food supply chain beyond the farm gate adds another layer of energy demand. Processing, packaging, transportation, and storage depend on reliable power supplies, particularly for perishable goods requiring refrigeration. Energy-efficient processing technologies, optimized logistics, and local food systems can reduce total energy use and emissions. In many developing economies, the lack of reliable energy access constrains food system development and increases post-harvest losses. Expanding renewable energy access in rural areas strengthens food security by improving storage, reducing waste, and enhancing economic opportunities.

Ecosystems themselves are influenced by energy demand and production patterns. Fossil fuel–based energy systems contribute to air and water pollution that degrade natural habitats, while renewable energy installations alter land and water use dynamics. Hydropower, for instance, offers a low-carbon energy source but can modify river flow regimes, affecting aquatic biodiversity and ecosystem services. Balancing energy development with ecosystem preservation requires careful planning and environmental safeguards. Integrated approaches that link energy, water, and ecosystem management ensure that energy expansion supports, rather than undermines, environmental objectives.

Climate systems also interact closely with energy demand across the Nexus. Rising temperatures increase cooling and irrigation needs, leading to higher energy consumption, particularly in urban and agricultural sectors. Extreme weather events disrupt energy infrastructure, affecting water supply, food storage, and ecosystem stability. The decarbonization of energy systems through renewable technologies reduces greenhouse gas emissions while decreasing long-term climate risks. However, the production and deployment of low-carbon technologies also carry embedded energy costs that must be considered in lifecycle assessments. Transitioning to a sustainable energy mix thus involves managing trade-offs between immediate efficiency gains and long-term system resilience.

Quantifying energy flows across the Nexus provides insights into interdependencies and potential efficiency gains. Energy audits and modeling approaches can identify hotspots of high energy intensity in water and food systems, guiding investment in technology and infrastructure improvements. Integrated assessment tools that link water, energy, and land data enable policymakers to analyze trade-offs between competing uses. For example, increasing irrigation efficiency can reduce both water and energy demand, while waste-to-energy initiatives in wastewater treatment can contribute to circular resource use.

Policy frameworks play a central role in addressing cross-sectoral energy demand. Energy pricing, subsidies, and regulation influence how water and food sectors consume power and adopt efficiency measures. In many countries, energy subsidies for irrigation or water pumping distort resource use by encouraging over-extraction. Reforming such subsidies to reflect environmental costs, combined with incentives for renewable energy integration, can promote more sustainable practices. National energy plans should be aligned with water and agricultural strategies to ensure coherence and avoid conflicting objectives.

Technological innovation underpins efforts to optimize energy use across sectors. Advances in digitalization, automation, and real-time monitoring enable precise control over energy consumption in water utilities and agricultural systems. Smart grids, coupled with distributed renewable energy generation, can enhance reliability and reduce losses. Hybrid systems combining solar, wind, and battery storage are increasingly being deployed in remote or water-scarce areas, providing resilient energy access while reducing dependency on fossil fuels.

Understanding energy demand across Nexus sectors highlights both the scale of interdependence and the opportunities for transformation. Managing these interconnections through integrated planning, technological innovation, and policy coherence can enhance overall system efficiency, reduce emissions, and strengthen resilience to climate and resource pressures. Recognizing energy as both a driver and a constraint within the WEFEC framework allows societies to design strategies that achieve sustainable resource security and equitable development across interconnected domains.

Renewable Energy Integration

The transition toward renewable energy is central to achieving sustainability across the WEFEC Nexus. Renewable energy sources such as solar, wind, geothermal, and bioenergy offer pathways to reduce greenhouse gas emissions, lower dependence on fossil fuels, and alleviate stress on water-intensive energy systems. Integrating these technologies requires coordinated planning to balance resource efficiency, environmental protection, and social equity. The process not only supports climate mitigation but also strengthens resilience across interconnected systems that depend on reliable and sustainable energy supplies.

Traditional fossil fuel–based energy production relies heavily on water for extraction, processing, and cooling. Thermal power plants, including coal, gas, and nuclear facilities, require significant volumes of freshwater, contributing to competition with agricultural and municipal users. In contrast, renewable energy technologies, particularly solar photovoltaics (PV) and wind, have minimal water requirements during operation. This shift reduces the overall water footprint of the energy sector while lowering vulnerability to water scarcity. Replacing water-intensive energy systems with low-water renewables thus contributes directly to both climate and water security goals.

Solar energy plays a vital role in diversifying the energy mix and reducing environmental impacts. Solar PV systems convert sunlight directly into electricity with no need for water-based cooling, making them suitable for arid and semi-arid regions where water is scarce. Concentrated solar power (CSP) systems, which use mirrors to focus sunlight to generate heat, require water for cooling but can adopt dry or hybrid cooling technologies to reduce consumption. Solar energy also supports decentralized applications such as off-grid irrigation systems and water desalination units, linking renewable energy deployment directly to food and water security within the Nexus framework.

Wind energy provides another major avenue for low-carbon power generation with minimal environmental footprint. Wind turbines consume negligible water during operation and have limited land-use conflicts when sited appropriately. Coastal and offshore wind farms harness consistent wind patterns, offering stable power output that complements solar generation. However, integrating variable wind energy into existing grids requires advancements in storage technologies and flexible grid management. Coordinated energy planning can ensure that intermittent renewable sources are balanced with dispatchable generation, maintaining reliability while minimizing overall system stress.

Bioenergy presents a more complex relationship within the Nexus due to its dual dependence on land and water resources. While bioenergy can support carbon neutrality by displacing fossil fuels, its production competes with food crops for land and irrigation water. The cultivation of biofuel feedstocks such as corn, sugarcane, and oilseed requires substantial inputs that may strain ecosystems if poorly managed. To align bioenergy with Nexus objectives, production systems must prioritize sustainable feedstocks, such as agricultural residues, waste biomass, and non-irrigated crops. Integrating bioenergy with circular economy principles—recovering nutrients, reusing water, and recycling waste—enhances resource efficiency and mitigates environmental trade-offs.

Hydropower remains a dominant renewable energy source globally, contributing to energy security and emission reduction. However, it also illustrates the interdependence of water and energy systems. Hydropower projects depend on consistent water flows, which are increasingly affected by climate change through altered precipitation and melting glaciers. Moreover, large-scale dams can disrupt ecosystems and modify downstream water availability. Optimizing hydropower's role within the Nexus involves improving operational efficiency, adopting environmental flow standards, and incorporating multi-purpose reservoir management to balance energy production with agricultural and ecological needs.

Integrating renewable energy into the broader resource system requires cross-sectoral coordination and supportive policy frameworks. Energy planning must account for interactions with water, agriculture, and ecosystems to prevent unintended consequences. Policies promoting renewable energy expansion can be strengthened by incorporating environmental impact assessments, land-use planning, and water management considerations. Financial incentives, carbon pricing, and public–private partnerships can accelerate renewable deployment while ensuring social and environmental safeguards. Regulatory alignment between energy and environmental authorities helps streamline decision-making and enhance sustainability outcomes.

Technological innovation supports the integration of renewables by improving storage, efficiency, and flexibility. Advances in battery technologies, hydrogen production, and smart grids allow renewable power to be harnessed more effectively and distributed reliably. Coupling renewable energy with water and agricultural systems— such as solar-powered irrigation, wind-assisted desalination, and waste-to-energy solutions—demonstrates the potential for synergistic resource use. Digital technologies, including artificial intelligence and data analytics, enhance system optimization by forecasting demand, managing variability, and ensuring efficient allocation of energy and water resources.

Social and economic factors also shape the pace of renewable energy integration. Expanding renewables creates opportunities for employment, rural development, and energy access, particularly in underserved regions. Decentralized renewable systems reduce dependence on centralized fossil fuel infrastructure, empowering local communities and enhancing energy equity. However, transition challenges include upfront costs, infrastructure adaptation, and the need for skilled labor. Addressing these barriers through targeted policy support, training programs, and financing mechanisms ensures that the energy transition delivers inclusive benefits across sectors.

Renewable energy integration represents a cornerstone of the Nexus approach, linking decarbonization with water conservation, food production, and ecosystem stability. Coordinated deployment of diverse renewable technologies enables societies to achieve multiple sustainability objectives simultaneously. By reducing water demand, mitigating emissions, and enhancing energy access, renewable integration provides a pathway toward a resilient and resource-efficient future aligned with global climate and development goals.

Energy-Water Trade-Offs

Energy and water systems are deeply interconnected, with each dependent on the other for operation and sustainability. Energy generation requires significant quantities of water for cooling, extraction, and processing, while water supply and treatment systems rely on energy to pump, distribute, and purify water. This interdependence creates trade-offs that can become acute under conditions of scarcity, growth in demand, or environmental stress. Understanding and managing these trade-offs is essential for

36

ensuring resource security and advancing integrated Nexus governance.

Desalination exemplifies the close relationship between energy and water. As global freshwater resources become increasingly constrained, desalination offers an alternative means of meeting water demand, particularly in arid and coastal regions. However, conventional desalination technologies, such as thermal distillation and reverse osmosis, are highly energy-intensive. Thermal processes rely on large amounts of heat, often generated from fossil fuels, while reverse osmosis requires substantial electrical energy to power high-pressure pumps. The energy intensity of desalination not only raises costs but also contributes to greenhouse gas emissions unless renewable energy is used. Efforts to reduce these impacts include integrating solar or wind energy into desalination plants, improving membrane efficiency, and adopting hybrid systems that combine multiple desalination methods for optimized performance.

Thermal power generation, including coal, gas, and nuclear plants, is another major source of water consumption. These plants require large quantities of water for cooling, accounting for a significant portion of industrial freshwater withdrawals worldwide. Cooling systems vary in their efficiency and environmental footprint; once-through systems withdraw large volumes but return much of the water to the environment, often at higher temperatures, while recirculating systems consume more water through evaporation but withdraw less overall. The choice of cooling technology therefore affects both local water availability and thermal pollution. Transitioning from water-intensive thermal generation to renewable energy sources reduces these dependencies, while improvements in cooling technologies—such as dry or hybrid systems—can further minimize water use in existing plants.

Biofuel production illustrates the complex and sometimes competing demands of energy and water systems. The cultivation of feedstock crops such as sugarcane, corn, or soybeans requires significant irrigation, fertilizers, and energy inputs. In regions with limited water availability, biofuel expansion can intensify competition with food production and ecosystems. Additionally, processing biofuels consumes additional water for fermentation and cooling. To mitigate these trade-offs, strategies include using non-irrigated or rainfed feedstocks, recycling process water, and prioritizing second-generation biofuels derived from agricultural residues or non-food biomass. These approaches reduce water demand while maintaining energy production capacity within sustainable limits.

The operation of hydropower plants introduces further complexities in the energy-water relationship. While hydropower is a renewable and low-emission energy source, its reliance on water availability makes it sensitive to climatic variability and competing uses. Extended droughts reduce generation capacity, while excessive reservoir releases during floods can affect downstream agricultural and ecological systems. Balancing hydropower generation with other water demands requires dynamic reservoir management, environmental flow standards, and integrated planning across sectors to avoid resource conflicts and ensure system reliability.

Industrial processes related to energy production also contribute to high water demand. Extractive industries such as coal mining, oil refining, and natural gas processing require water for washing, cooling, and chemical treatment. Hydraulic fracturing (fracking) operations in particular use large volumes of water mixed with chemicals to release gas and oil from shale formations. These activities not only increase water demand but also pose risks of contamination to surface and groundwater. Implementing closed-loop systems, recycling produced water, and enforcing strict environmental safeguards can mitigate the negative impacts of these operations on local water systems.

The relationship between energy and water is further shaped by climate change. Rising temperatures and shifting precipitation patterns affect both water availability and energy demand. Increased cooling requirements in warmer climates raise energy use, while droughts limit water supplies for hydropower and thermal plants. Conversely, energy-intensive water management measures such as desalination and inter-basin transfers can increase emissions, creating feedback loops that reinforce climate pressures. Managing these interactions requires integrated adaptation strategies that align water and energy planning under shared climate resilience goals.

Reducing energy-water trade-offs involves technological innovation, system efficiency, and coordinated governance. On the technology front, advances in low-energy desalination, wastewater reuse, and closed-loop cooling systems are reducing energy and water footprints across sectors. Energy recovery systems in water treatment plants and hybrid renewable-powered desalination are expanding practical solutions for sustainable operations. From a governance perspective, aligning water and energy policies ensures that resource allocation decisions reflect interdependencies rather than isolated objectives. Cross-sectoral planning frameworks, supported by data sharing and joint monitoring, facilitate evidence-based management of shared resources.

Integrated planning and innovation together offer pathways to minimize trade-offs and enhance synergies within the WEFEC Nexus. By designing policies that balance resource efficiency with environmental protection, societies can reduce the pressure on both water and energy systems. Coordinated strategies—combining renewable energy deployment, improved water efficiency, and adaptive infrastructure—create the conditions for long-term sustainability and resilience in a changing climate.

Energy Governance and Transition Pathways

Energy governance defines the institutional, regulatory, and policy mechanisms that guide how societies produce, distribute, and consume energy. In the context of the WEFEC Nexus, governance frameworks determine the balance between sustainability and economic growth. Transitioning to low-carbon energy systems requires coherent policies that align national energy goals with water management, food production, and ecosystem protection. Coordinated governance ensures that energy transitions support resource efficiency, climate resilience, and social equity across interconnected systems.

National energy transitions are driven by the need to decarbonize economies, reduce reliance on fossil fuels, and integrate renewable energy sources. These transitions influence water and food systems by altering patterns of resource use, land demand, and emissions. The development of renewable energy infrastructure, for example, affects land availability for agriculture and may alter water flows or biodiversity. Policymakers must consider these cross-sectoral interactions to avoid unintended trade-offs. Governance frameworks that adopt a Nexus approach can ensure that energy policies contribute to sustainable resource use and climate objectives.

Effective governance for energy transition relies on integrated policy design. Traditional energy governance has often been fragmented, with separate institutions managing generation, regulation, and environmental compliance. Such structures create policy gaps that hinder systemic efficiency. Integrated governance frameworks promote collaboration among ministries responsible for energy, water, agriculture, and environment, allowing for unified planning and shared monitoring systems. This coordination supports policies that optimize resource use and prevent conflicts. For example, aligning renewable energy expansion with water and agricultural policies can reduce pressure on freshwater resources while maintaining food security.

Regulatory reform is a key enabler of successful energy transitions. Governments must adapt regulations to encourage investment in renewable energy, modernize grids, and phase out inefficient fossil fuel subsidies. At the same time, policies must safeguard water resources, ecosystems, and food production. Environmental impact assessments, energy pricing mechanisms, and resource efficiency standards ensure that economic growth aligns with sustainability. Introducing carbon pricing or emissions trading systems internalizes environmental costs and stimulates innovation in clean technologies. Transparent and predictable regulation fosters investor confidence while maintaining accountability and environmental protection.

Decentralized governance plays an important role in supporting localized energy transitions. Distributed renewable energy systems, such as rooftop solar or community wind projects, allow regions to tailor energy strategies to their unique resource conditions. Local authorities can develop context-specific policies that integrate water and agricultural needs with energy planning. Empowering local institutions enhances resilience by diversifying energy sources and reducing dependence on centralized fossil fuel infrastructure. However, decentralization requires strong coordination with national frameworks to ensure consistency in technical standards, financing, and long-term objectives.

International cooperation complements national governance by promoting knowledge sharing, technology transfer, and financial support for clean energy projects. Global frameworks such as the Paris Agreement provide structure for aligning national contributions toward emission reductions. Multilateral development banks and climate funds play an essential role in financing transitions in developing economies. Collaborative initiatives—ranging from renewable energy partnerships to cross-border grid interconnections—enhance energy security and efficiency. Participation in global networks also enables countries to learn from best practices and adapt successful models to local conditions.

Institutional capacity is another determinant of effective energy governance. Transitioning to low-carbon systems requires skilled professionals, data infrastructure, and technical expertise across all levels of administration. Training programs for policymakers and regulators improve understanding of the interconnections within the Nexus. Data integration platforms support decision-making by linking information on energy demand, water availability, and climate impacts. Building institutional capacity ensures that energy transitions are informed, adaptive, and capable of responding to emerging challenges.

Stakeholder engagement strengthens governance by ensuring inclusivity and accountability. Energy transitions affect a wide range of actors—governments, industries, communities, and consumers—

each with distinct interests and capacities. Participatory decision-making builds trust and fosters social acceptance of new technologies and policy reforms. Mechanisms such as consultation forums, public hearings, and stakeholder partnerships encourage dialogue and transparency. Engaging non-state actors, including private investors and civil society, enhances innovation and resource mobilization while ensuring that policies reflect diverse perspectives.

Financing is central to implementing transition pathways. Mobilizing investment in renewable energy, grid modernization, and energy efficiency requires blended finance mechanisms that combine public funds, private capital, and international support. Green bonds, climate funds, and public–private partnerships can accelerate deployment while maintaining fiscal sustainability. Governance frameworks must establish clear guidelines for financial accountability and risk management to attract investment and ensure equitable benefits distribution.

Energy transition pathways must be adaptive and forward-looking. Rapid technological advances, market shifts, and climate impacts demand flexible policies capable of evolving over time. Scenario planning, regular policy reviews, and iterative governance processes allow for adjustment to emerging opportunities and constraints. Integrating climate adaptation into energy planning ensures that infrastructure and systems remain resilient under future environmental conditions.

Energy governance within the WEFEC Nexus therefore extends beyond managing energy supply—it encompasses the coordination of policies, institutions, and investments that sustain interconnected resource systems. Transition pathways grounded in integrated governance principles enable societies to move toward low-carbon, resource-efficient, and equitable energy futures.

Chapter 4: Food Security and Sustainable Agriculture

Food systems lie at the heart of the WEFEC Nexus, relying on water for irrigation, energy for processing and transport, and ecosystems for soil fertility and pollination. Agricultural practices both depend on and influence the stability of water and energy systems, while also shaping land use and greenhouse gas emissions. As climate change intensifies, ensuring food security requires transforming agricultural systems to become more resource-efficient, resilient, and environmentally sustainable. Understanding how food production interacts with water, energy, ecosystems, and climate enables policymakers and producers to design strategies that balance productivity with conservation.

Agricultural Resource Intensity

Agriculture remains one of the most resource-intensive sectors in the global economy, exerting substantial pressure on water, energy, and land systems. As the human population expands and dietary patterns shift toward higher consumption of resource-demanding foods, the demand for agricultural production continues to grow. This increase places additional strain on freshwater availability, soil fertility, and energy supplies, making the agricultural sector a central focus within the WEFEC Nexus. Understanding the patterns and drivers of agricultural resource intensity is essential for designing strategies that enhance productivity while reducing environmental impacts and ensuring long-term sustainability.

Water use in agriculture is particularly significant, accounting for nearly 70 percent of global freshwater withdrawals. Irrigation sustains crop yields in many regions, but it also leads to inefficiencies through evaporation, seepage, and over-application. Traditional flood irrigation methods, still widely used in developing regions, result in substantial water losses and soil salinization. These inefficiencies exacerbate water scarcity, especially in arid and semi-arid zones. The shift toward more efficient irrigation techniques, such as drip and sprinkler systems, offers a way to optimize water use by delivering it directly to plant roots, minimizing waste. Advances in sensor technology and data analytics further enable precision irrigation, where water applications are tailored to real-time crop and soil conditions, reducing both consumption and energy demand for pumping.

Energy use in agriculture is closely tied to water management, mechanization, and chemical inputs. Energy powers irrigation pumps, tractors, processing facilities, and cold storage systems that ensure food availability across supply chains. The energy demand of agriculture varies widely depending on production systems, crop types, and mechanization levels. Fossil fuels remain the dominant energy source for most agricultural operations, contributing to greenhouse gas emissions and exposing farmers to energy price fluctuations. Transitioning to renewable energy, such as solar-powered irrigation and biomass energy for rural processing, can reduce operational costs and environmental footprints. The integration of decentralized renewable systems also enhances energy access in remote farming areas, contributing to rural development and resilience.

Land use and crop selection are critical determinants of agricultural resource intensity. Monoculture systems, while maximizing short-term yields, often lead to soil degradation, biodiversity loss, and increased dependency on synthetic fertilizers and pesticides. Crop diversification and rotation improve soil health, enhance nutrient cycling, and reduce vulnerability to pests and diseases. Integrating legumes, for example, enriches soil nitrogen naturally, lowering the need for chemical fertilizers that are energy-intensive to produce. Mixed farming systems that combine crops, livestock, and trees (agroforestry) optimize resource use by creating complementary relationships between components. Such diversification aligns with Nexus principles by promoting resilience, reducing inputs, and stabilizing yields under variable climatic conditions.

Fertilizer and pesticide use contribute significantly to both energy and environmental intensity. The production of synthetic fertilizers is highly energy-dependent, particularly nitrogen fertilizers synthesized through the Haber–Bosch process. Excessive application of fertilizers not only increases energy consumption but also leads to nutrient runoff, contaminating water bodies and contributing to greenhouse gas emissions through nitrous oxide release. Precision agriculture techniques help optimize fertilizer use by applying nutrients in the right amount, at the right time, and in the right place. This targeted approach maintains productivity while minimizing environmental damage and reducing embedded energy demand.

Agricultural water and energy use are further influenced by climatic variability and ecosystem dynamics. Climate change alters precipitation patterns and temperature regimes, affecting irrigation demand and energy use for temperature regulation and pumping. Ecosystem degradation—such as deforestation, wetland loss, and soil erosion—reduces the natural capacity of landscapes to retain water and nutrients, intensifying reliance on artificial inputs. Maintaining healthy ecosystems through conservation agriculture, cover cropping, and soil organic matter management enhances natural water retention and carbon sequestration, decreasing the need for external inputs. These measures create feedback benefits across the Nexus by improving water efficiency, reducing energy consumption, and strengthening climate resilience.

Technology and data innovation offer transformative potential for reducing agricultural resource intensity. Remote sensing, satellite monitoring, and digital farm management tools enable real-time tracking of soil moisture, crop health, and weather conditions. By integrating these data sources, farmers can make informed decisions on irrigation scheduling, fertilization, and harvesting. Automation and precision machinery improve efficiency by minimizing waste and optimizing energy use. At the policy level, supporting access to technology through financing, training, and extension services ensures equitable adoption across regions, preventing the deepening of disparities between industrialized and smallholder systems.

Institutional and economic frameworks influence how efficiently agricultural resources are managed. Subsidies for water, energy, and fertilizers often encourage overuse, distorting true resource costs. Reforming these policies to promote efficiency and sustainability can create strong incentives for conservation. Payment schemes for ecosystem services, such as watershed protection or carbon sequestration, can reward farmers for practices that benefit broader environmental objectives. Integrating agricultural policy with water and energy governance strengthens coherence, aligning production incentives with sustainable resource use goals.

Reducing agricultural resource intensity is not merely a technical challenge but a systemic one requiring coordinated action across sectors and scales. The adoption of efficient irrigation, renewable energy technologies, precision farming, and diversified cropping systems collectively supports sustainable productivity. Aligning agricultural policies with the broader WEFEC Nexus ensures that gains in one sector do not come at the expense of another. By optimizing water and energy use while protecting ecosystems, agriculture can transition from a resource-intensive to a resource-efficient foundation for global food security.

Climate Impacts on Food Systems

Climate change is exerting growing pressure on global food systems by altering temperature patterns, precipitation cycles, and the frequency of extreme weather events. These changes disrupt agricultural productivity, supply chains, and food security, challenging the stability of economies and livelihoods. The WEFEC Nexus provides an integrated framework for understanding and managing these interactions, highlighting the need for adaptation strategies that strengthen resilience across interconnected systems.

Rising temperatures directly affect crop physiology, soil moisture, and pest dynamics. Many staple crops, including wheat, maize, and rice, have specific temperature thresholds beyond which yields decline sharply. Warmer conditions accelerate evapotranspiration, increasing water demand and reducing soil moisture availability. Prolonged heat stress can also impair pollination and seed development, leading to lower productivity and quality. Additionally, higher temperatures expand the geographical range of pests and diseases, exposing crops to new risks and reducing the effectiveness of traditional control measures. Livestock systems are similarly affected, as heat stress lowers feed efficiency, fertility, and milk production. Managing these temperature-related challenges requires adaptive crop selection, improved breeding for heat tolerance, and enhanced resource efficiency.

Precipitation variability further compounds the challenges of food production. Erratic rainfall patterns cause both drought and flooding, affecting soil health, irrigation scheduling, and crop yields. In many regions, the onset and duration of rainy seasons are becoming less predictable, disrupting planting cycles and increasing the likelihood of crop failure. Drought reduces groundwater recharge and surface water availability, forcing farmers to rely on energy-intensive irrigation or to leave fields fallow. Conversely, excessive rainfall leads to waterlogging, soil erosion, and nutrient loss. The intensity of precipitation events also increases the risk of flooding that can damage infrastructure and contaminate water supplies. Adaptive water management, including rainwater harvesting, efficient irrigation, and watershed restoration, helps buffer food systems against these climatic extremes.

Climate change also disrupts the energy flows that sustain food systems. Higher temperatures and unreliable water supplies raise energy demand for irrigation, cooling, and transportation. Extreme weather can damage energy infrastructure, leading to power shortages that affect food storage and processing. These disruptions can ripple through supply chains, increasing post-harvest losses and food prices. Integrating renewable energy solutions into agriculture, such as solar-powered irrigation or decentralized cold storage, enhances resilience by providing reliable and sustainable power sources. Efficient energy use throughout production and distribution reduces costs and emissions while strengthening system stability under variable climate conditions.

The impacts of climate change on ecosystems further influence food production. Degraded ecosystems lose their capacity to regulate water flows, support pollinators, and maintain soil fertility. Deforestation, wetland loss, and soil degradation diminish the ecological foundations of food systems, making them more vulnerable to climate stress. Extreme events such as wildfires and droughts can trigger cascading effects, reducing biodiversity and altering hydrological cycles that underpin agriculture. Restoring and protecting natural ecosystems through conservation agriculture, agroforestry, and sustainable land management helps maintain ecological functions essential for food security.

Climate-induced disruptions to global and regional food supply chains pose additional risks. Extreme weather events, including floods, storms, and droughts, can damage transportation infrastructure and reduce the availability of critical inputs such as seeds, fertilizers, and animal feed. Trade disruptions amplify price volatility, affecting both producers and consumers. Smallholder farmers, who often lack access to insurance, credit, or market diversification, are particularly exposed to these shocks. Strengthening local food systems through diversification, storage infrastructure, and adaptive logistics improves resilience and reduces dependency on vulnerable trade networks.

Adaptation practices within the WEFEC Nexus framework offer pathways to mitigate climate impacts on food systems. Integrated approaches combine water management, energy efficiency, and ecosystem restoration to support sustainable agricultural productivity. Precision agriculture technologies optimize input use under changing climate conditions, while climate-smart agriculture promotes practices that enhance soil health, conserve water, and reduce emissions. Diversified production systems, including crop rotation and mixed farming, spread risk and increase resilience to climate variability. Policy interventions that link agricultural planning with climate adaptation strategies ensure that investments address systemic vulnerabilities rather than isolated problems.

The governance of food systems under climate stress requires cross-sectoral coordination and proactive planning. Agricultural, water, and energy policies must align to manage resource trade-offs and optimize synergies. Investment in research and development of resilient crop varieties, efficient irrigation technologies, and renewable energy integration is critical to support adaptation. Financial instruments such as climate insurance and risk-sharing mechanisms can protect farmers from losses and encourage adoption of sustainable practices. Strengthening data systems and early warning mechanisms further enables timely responses to climate risks, reducing the likelihood of production shocks.

The combined effects of temperature rise, rainfall variability, and ecosystem degradation underscore the need for holistic solutions that link food security with environmental sustainability. Addressing climate impacts on food systems requires systemic adaptation that integrates technological innovation, policy coherence, and inclusive governance. Within the WEFEC Nexus, resilience depends on the capacity to manage interconnections among resources, ensuring that agricultural development supports both human well-being and planetary health.

Ecosystem-Based Agriculture

Ecosystem-based agriculture integrates natural processes and ecosystem services into farming systems to enhance productivity, biodiversity, and resilience. This approach shifts the focus from maximizing short-term yields through intensive inputs to optimizing ecological functions that sustain long-term productivity. It recognizes that ecosystems provide critical services such as nutrient cycling, soil formation, water filtration, pest control, and pollination—all essential for food production. Incorporating these natural functions into agricultural management aligns food systems with environmental sustainability and strengthens their capacity to adapt to climate variability within the WEFEC Nexus.

Soil health is the foundation of ecosystem-based agriculture. Healthy soils store carbon, retain water, and support microbial life that recycles nutrients for plant growth. Intensive farming practices, including excessive tillage and chemical fertilizer use, degrade soil structure and reduce organic matter, undermining long-term fertility. Conservation tillage, organic amendments, and crop rotations that include legumes enhance soil organic carbon and microbial diversity. These practices increase nutrient availability, improve water infiltration, and reduce erosion. By strengthening soil's ecological functions, farmers can maintain productivity while reducing dependence on synthetic fertilizers and irrigation.

Biodiversity plays a vital role in maintaining resilient agricultural systems. A diverse mix of crops, livestock, and natural habitats supports ecological interactions that regulate pests, enhance pollination, and buffer against disease outbreaks. Habitat corridors, field margins, and agroforestry systems provide shelter and resources for beneficial species such as pollinators and natural predators. Biodiversity also increases system stability by spreading risk—diverse crops respond differently to stressors such as drought, pests, or temperature extremes. Genetic diversity within crop species ensures adaptability to changing environmental conditions. Maintaining and enhancing on-farm biodiversity strengthens the ecological foundation of agricultural productivity while conserving ecosystem integrity.

Water management in ecosystem-based agriculture emphasizes efficiency, retention, and natural hydrological functions. Restoring wetlands, maintaining riparian buffers, and employing contour farming reduce runoff and enhance groundwater recharge. These measures stabilize local hydrology, moderate flood and drought impacts, and improve water quality by filtering sediments and pollutants. Incorporating perennial vegetation in agricultural landscapes further supports water regulation by reducing evaporation and promoting infiltration. Combining these natural processes with efficient irrigation technologies, such as drip systems and soil moisture sensors, ensures that water use aligns with both agricultural and ecological needs.

Nutrient management under ecosystem-based approaches focuses on recycling and minimizing losses. Instead of relying solely on external inputs, systems integrate composting, green manures, and livestock manure to maintain soil fertility. Cover crops fix atmospheric nitrogen and scavenge residual nutrients, preventing leaching into waterways. Integrating crop and livestock operations creates closed nutrient loops that mimic natural cycles, reducing pollution and improving resource efficiency. These practices also contribute to climate mitigation by increasing carbon sequestration in soils and biomass. Nutrient recycling aligns with circular economy principles and reinforces sustainability within the WEFEC Nexus by linking food production to ecosystem regeneration.

Pest and disease control in ecosystem-based agriculture relies on ecological balance rather than chemical intervention. Diversified cropping systems, intercropping, and crop rotations disrupt pest life cycles and reduce the buildup of pathogens. Biological control using natural predators and parasitoids maintains pest populations below damaging levels. Maintaining ecological infrastructure, such as hedgerows and flower strips, provides habitats for beneficial organisms. Reduced pesticide use protects soil biota and pollinators, supporting both ecosystem health and agricultural productivity. Integrating these biological and cultural methods enhances resilience to pest outbreaks while minimizing environmental contamination.

Ecosystem-based agriculture also contributes to climate regulation through carbon sequestration and reduced emissions. Practices such as agroforestry, conservation tillage, and cover cropping store carbon in soil and vegetation. Perennial crops and trees capture atmospheric carbon dioxide over long timeframes, while reduced soil disturbance limits the release of stored carbon. These actions help mitigate climate change while improving soil fertility and water retention. By maintaining vegetative cover, ecosystem-based systems also moderate local microclimates, reducing heat stress on crops and livestock. Integrating agriculture with ecosystem restoration therefore supports both mitigation and adaptation goals within the climate dimension of the Nexus.

Technology and innovation play a supportive role in implementing ecosystem-based approaches. Remote sensing, geographic information systems, and data analytics help monitor soil health, water use, and biodiversity across landscapes. Digital tools enable adaptive management by providing real-time data on ecosystem conditions and resource flows. Combining traditional knowledge with modern technology ensures locally appropriate and scalable solutions. Policies that incentivize ecosystem-based practices through payments for ecosystem services, certification programs, and sustainability standards can accelerate adoption. Institutional collaboration between agricultural, environmental, and water agencies promotes coordinated management that reflects Nexus principles.

Ecosystem-based agriculture represents a shift toward farming systems that regenerate rather than deplete natural resources. By embedding ecological processes into food production, it reconciles the objectives of productivity, environmental stewardship, and climate resilience. Within the WEFEC framework, such approaches illustrate how human-managed landscapes can function as integral components of healthy ecosystems that sustain both people and the planet.

Circular and Resource-Efficient Food Systems

Circular and resource-efficient food systems apply the principles of reducing waste, reusing by-products, and recycling nutrients to optimize resource use across the entire value chain. They represent a transition from the traditional linear model of "take, make, and dispose" toward systems that regenerate natural capital and maintain materials within productive cycles. Within the WEFEC Nexus, circular food systems enhance sustainability by minimizing environmental footprints, conserving resources, and strengthening the resilience of both ecosystems and communities.

The foundation of circular food systems lies in closing resource loops. Each stage of food production—from cultivation and processing to consumption and disposal—presents opportunities to recover and reuse materials that would otherwise become waste. For example, agricultural residues can serve as raw materials for bioenergy production, animal feed, or compost. Similarly, organic waste from households and industries can be converted into biogas or organic fertilizers, returning nutrients to the soil. These processes reduce dependency on synthetic inputs, lower greenhouse gas emissions, and enhance soil fertility. Designing systems that recapture value at each stage requires collaboration across supply chains and supportive policy frameworks that incentivize circular practices.

Resource efficiency is achieved by optimizing the inputs required for food production. Water and energy efficiency play crucial roles in this context. Advanced irrigation systems, such as precision drip irrigation, reduce water use while maintaining yields. Integrating renewable energy into food production—through solar-powered pumps, biogas digesters, or wind turbines—reduces fossil fuel consumption and operational costs. Circularity also extends to reducing energy losses throughout processing, storage, and transportation by improving insulation, logistics, and refrigeration efficiency. The combination of technological innovation and systems-level coordination ensures that inputs are used sustainably and outputs are valorized rather than wasted.

Nutrient cycling is a central element of circular food systems. Traditional agricultural systems often rely on mineral fertilizers produced from finite resources, such as phosphorus and nitrogen derived from industrial processes. These inputs can leach into water bodies, causing eutrophication and ecosystem degradation. Circular nutrient management focuses on recovering nutrients from organic waste, wastewater, and agricultural residues. Composting, anaerobic digestion, and nutrient recovery technologies transform waste streams into valuable soil amendments and bio-based fertilizers. Integrating these approaches within urban and rural settings creates localized nutrient cycles, reducing pollution and enhancing soil health. This nutrient circularity not only supports agricultural productivity but also strengthens water quality and ecosystem integrity.

Food waste reduction across supply chains is another pillar of circularity. Globally, approximately one-third of all food produced is lost or wasted, representing a significant waste of water, energy, and land resources. Addressing this issue requires interventions at multiple levels: improving post-harvest handling, upgrading storage and transportation infrastructure, and fostering consumer awareness. Technological solutions, including cold chains and digital monitoring systems, help reduce spoilage. Policy measures that encourage redistribution of surplus food or the conversion of unavoidable waste into valuable by-products, such as bioenergy or animal feed, further enhance efficiency. Reducing food loss directly supports water and energy conservation while lowering emissions associated with waste decomposition.

Packaging innovation also contributes to circularity within food systems. Conventional packaging materials, particularly plastics, pose major environmental challenges. The development of biodegradable and recyclable materials, along with reusable packaging systems, reduces pollution and resource depletion. Circular packaging design emphasizes material recovery and reuse, aligning production with the principles of a closed-loop economy. Implementing extended producer responsibility schemes ensures that manufacturers remain accountable for the environmental impacts of their packaging throughout its lifecycle.

Digitalization supports circular and resource-efficient food systems by improving data-driven decision-making and transparency. Digital platforms enable tracking of resource flows, waste generation, and product origins. Blockchain technology can facilitate traceability, ensuring accountability across supply chains and reducing inefficiencies. Artificial intelligence and big data analytics help optimize logistics, predict demand, and minimize overproduction. These technologies enhance coordination among producers, processors, retailers, and consumers, enabling the creation of interconnected food systems that are adaptive, efficient, and resilient.

Governance and policy frameworks are essential to scaling circular food systems. Governments can promote resource efficiency through regulations, incentives, and research funding. Policies that encourage waste separation, recycling infrastructure, and renewable energy integration foster an enabling environment for circular practices. Public–private partnerships can mobilize investment in circular technologies and infrastructure. International cooperation further facilitates knowledge exchange and harmonization of standards, enabling consistent implementation of circularity across borders.

Circular food systems also depend on behavioral and cultural change. Consumers play a vital role in reducing food waste, choosing sustainable products, and supporting recycling initiatives. Education campaigns, labeling schemes, and incentives for responsible consumption help foster a circular mindset. Community-based initiatives such as urban composting and local food cooperatives strengthen engagement and awareness. Embedding circular principles in education and training ensures that future generations are equipped to sustain these practices.

Transitioning to circular and resource-efficient food systems aligns directly with the broader goals of the WEFEC Nexus. By reducing waste, conserving water and energy, recycling nutrients, and protecting ecosystems, circularity transforms food systems into engines of sustainability. The integration of circular practices across production, consumption, and governance not only enhances resource efficiency but also advances global objectives of food security, climate mitigation, and environmental regeneration.

Chapter 5: Ecosystems and Biodiversity in the Nexus

Ecosystems and biodiversity form the foundation of the WEFEC Nexus, providing the natural capital that sustains resource cycles and human well-being. Forests, wetlands, and soils regulate water flows, store carbon, and support nutrient cycles that underpin food and energy production. Biodiversity enhances ecosystem stability, enabling adaptive responses to disturbances such as droughts and floods. Yet, land-use change, pollution, and climate stress continue to degrade ecosystems and erode biodiversity, weakening their capacity to deliver essential services. Integrating ecosystem and biodiversity considerations into Nexus strategies is vital for maintaining long-term resilience and sustainability across all sectors.

Ecosystem Services Supporting Nexus Functions

Ecosystems sustain the WEFEC Nexus by providing essential services that regulate, support, and enhance human and natural systems. These services form the foundation for resource availability, productivity, and resilience. They operate through complex interactions that influence water purification, nutrient cycling, soil fertility, carbon storage, and biodiversity maintenance. Recognizing and managing ecosystem services as integral components of the Nexus ensures that resource management and development strategies are aligned with environmental integrity and long-term sustainability.

Regulating services are central to ecosystem contributions within the Nexus. Wetlands, forests, and grasslands regulate water flows, filter pollutants, and mitigate floods and droughts. Vegetated landscapes act as natural sponges, absorbing rainfall and recharging groundwater aquifers while moderating runoff that can cause erosion or sedimentation. Forest canopies intercept precipitation, reducing surface flow and maintaining base flows in rivers during dry periods. Similarly, riparian zones trap sediments and nutrients, improving water quality downstream. These regulating processes reduce reliance on built infrastructure such as dams and water treatment plants. By maintaining hydrological balance, ecosystems enhance water security and support energy and food systems dependent on reliable freshwater supplies.

Carbon storage and climate regulation represent another vital ecosystem function. Forests, wetlands, peatlands, and marine ecosystems act as major carbon sinks, capturing and storing atmospheric carbon dioxide. This process mitigates climate change by reducing the concentration of greenhouse gases and stabilizing global temperatures. Vegetation and soils together store more carbon than the atmosphere, highlighting their significance in climate regulation. When these ecosystems are degraded or converted to other land uses, stored carbon is released, contributing to emissions. Maintaining and restoring natural carbon sinks through afforestation, reforestation, and soil management strengthens climate resilience across the Nexus. Climate-regulating services also include temperature moderation and local microclimate stabilization, which influence agricultural productivity and water availability.

Provisioning services provide direct material benefits that sustain human well-being and economic activity. Ecosystems supply freshwater for domestic, industrial, and agricultural use, as well as raw materials such as timber, fuelwood, and non-timber forest products. Fisheries and rangelands provide protein and livelihoods, while fertile soils underpin food production. Many of these resources are renewable only if ecosystems remain intact and functional. Overexploitation, pollution, and land-use change can disrupt these provisioning capacities, leading to resource depletion and loss of resilience. Sustainable management of provisioning services requires balancing short-term extraction with long-term regeneration to maintain ecosystem productivity within safe ecological limits.

Cultural services represent the social and aesthetic dimensions of ecosystems that support human identity, heritage, and mental well-being. Landscapes, rivers, and forests often hold spiritual, recreational, and educational value. Access to natural spaces improves physical and psychological health, supports tourism, and fosters cultural traditions linked to land and water stewardship. Recognizing the cultural dimension of ecosystem services helps integrate social values into resource management and policy. When communities are involved in conserving culturally significant ecosystems, they develop a stronger sense of ownership and responsibility, enhancing stewardship and sustainability outcomes.

Supporting services form the ecological foundation upon which all other ecosystem functions depend. Processes such as photosynthesis, nutrient cycling, and soil formation sustain the production of biomass and maintain the structure of living systems. Microbial activity in soils decomposes organic matter, releasing nutrients essential for plant growth. Pollinators enable reproduction for many crops and wild plants, ensuring food production and biodiversity continuity. Wetlands and coastal ecosystems facilitate nutrient and sediment cycling that supports fisheries and agricultural fertility. Without these supporting processes, the stability of provisioning, regulating, and cultural services would decline, weakening the resilience of the Nexus as a whole.

Ecosystem services also mediate trade-offs and synergies within the Nexus. For instance, increasing agricultural land at the expense of forests may enhance short-term food supply but reduce carbon storage, water regulation, and biodiversity. Conversely, maintaining wetlands can enhance water purification and flood protection but may reduce land available for cultivation. Managing these trade-offs requires integrated approaches that recognize the multi-functional nature of ecosystems. By quantifying and valuing ecosystem services, decision-makers can identify co-benefits across sectors and design policies that optimize multiple outcomes simultaneously. Tools such as ecosystem accounting and spatial mapping help visualize interconnections, supporting informed and balanced resource management.

Economic valuation of ecosystem services plays a critical role in mainstreaming them into decision-making. Traditionally, ecosystem functions have been undervalued or treated as externalities, leading to overexploitation and degradation. Valuation approaches—ranging from market-based mechanisms to non-market assessments—help quantify the benefits ecosystems provide in economic terms. Payment for ecosystem services (PES) schemes compensate landowners or communities for maintaining ecological functions, creating financial incentives for conservation. Integrating ecosystem values into national accounting systems ensures that natural capital is considered alongside financial and manufactured assets, aligning economic planning with environmental sustainability.

Governance frameworks that support ecosystem services management require coordination across sectors, jurisdictions, and scales. Policies must reconcile competing demands for land, water, and energy while protecting ecological integrity. Cross-sectoral institutions can facilitate dialogue among stakeholders in agriculture, forestry, energy, and water management. Legal mechanisms such as protected areas, watershed management plans, and environmental regulations safeguard critical ecosystems that underpin Nexus functions. Adaptive governance—built on monitoring, feedback, and stakeholder participation—ensures that management strategies remain responsive to ecological and social changes.

Ecosystem services underpin the stability, productivity, and adaptability of the WEFEC Nexus. Their preservation ensures the continuous functioning of resource systems that sustain economies and societies. Integrating these services into policy and planning strengthens the resilience of natural and human systems to environmental change, securing the foundations of sustainable development.

Land-Use Change and Resource Competition

Land-use change lies at the intersection of environmental sustainability and development, shaping the availability and quality of water, energy, food, and ecosystem resources. As populations expand and economies grow, demand for land intensifies, leading to the conversion of forests, wetlands, and grasslands into agricultural fields, urban areas, and energy infrastructure. These shifts alter biophysical processes, disrupt ecosystems, and intensify competition among sectors. Within the WEFEC Nexus, managing land use equitably and strategically is crucial to maintaining resource balance and ensuring long-term resilience.

Agricultural expansion remains one of the leading drivers of land-use change. As food demand rises with population growth and changing diets, the pressure to convert natural landscapes into cropland or pasture increases. This expansion often comes at the cost of forests and wetlands, which serve as key carbon sinks and biodiversity reservoirs. Clearing vegetation for agriculture reduces soil stability, increases erosion, and alters hydrological cycles, diminishing the capacity of ecosystems to store and filter water. Furthermore, monoculture cropping systems intensify nutrient runoff and pesticide pollution, contributing to water degradation downstream. Sustainable intensification—producing more food from existing farmland without environmental harm—offers a path to decouple food production from land conversion.

Energy infrastructure development, including biofuel plantations, hydropower reservoirs, and renewable energy installations, adds another layer of land-use competition. Biofuel crops such as maize and sugarcane compete directly with food production for arable land and water, raising concerns about food security and biodiversity. Large-scale hydropower dams alter river ecosystems and flood fertile valleys, while solar and wind farms require land allocation that can displace agricultural or ecological areas. Integrating energy planning with land and water management minimizes these conflicts by promoting co-location strategies and multi-use landscapes. For example, agrivoltaic systems, which combine solar power generation with agricultural activities, exemplify synergistic land use that supports both energy and food security goals.

Urbanization and infrastructure expansion significantly reshape land-use dynamics. Cities concentrate populations and economic activity but often spread outward into surrounding agricultural or natural areas. This expansion leads to habitat fragmentation, reduced green space, and increased surface runoff, which degrades water quality and intensifies flood risks. Urban growth also heightens competition for water and energy, drawing resources away from rural production systems. Adopting compact urban designs, integrated land-use zoning, and green infrastructure can mitigate these pressures. Urban planning that incorporates nature-based solutions—such as urban wetlands, green corridors, and permeable surfaces—helps retain ecosystem functionality within expanding metropolitan regions.

Deforestation and land degradation are closely linked to resource competition. Clearing forests for agriculture, timber, and mining releases stored carbon and reduces the landscape's ability to regulate water and climate. Deforestation disrupts local rainfall patterns, increases soil erosion, and contributes to biodiversity loss, which undermines ecosystem services vital for agriculture and water systems. Land degradation, including desertification and salinization, further reduces productivity and drives migration and poverty. Restoring degraded land through reforestation, soil rehabilitation, and sustainable land management practices restores ecological balance while enhancing carbon sequestration and water retention. Integrating restoration into national development policies strengthens ecosystem resilience and mitigates trade-offs among sectors.

Water scarcity intensifies resource competition under changing land-use patterns. Irrigated agriculture, industrial development, and energy production all require substantial water inputs, while land conversion reduces natural infiltration and recharge. Over-extraction of groundwater for farming or urban use leads to depletion and declining water quality. Similarly, land compaction and loss of vegetation diminish watershed functionality, increasing runoff and flood risk. Strategic land-use planning that preserves critical recharge zones, riparian buffers, and wetlands ensures that water systems continue to support both human and ecological needs. Spatial planning tools such as hydrological mapping and ecosystem service assessments can guide land-use decisions toward maintaining water balance.

Climate change amplifies the consequences of land-use change by altering precipitation patterns, temperature regimes, and vegetation dynamics. Droughts and floods affect land productivity, prompting shifts in agricultural zones and intensifying pressure on remaining fertile areas. Climate-induced migration may increase urban encroachment and competition for land resources. Integrating climate adaptation into land-use planning helps anticipate and manage these transitions. Climate-resilient landscapes—comprising diverse ecosystems, managed forests, and restored wetlands—buffer against extreme weather events and provide stable foundations for agriculture and energy systems.

Governance and policy coordination are essential to addressing land-use competition across sectors. Fragmented institutional responsibilities often result in conflicting objectives for agriculture, energy, and conservation. Integrated land-use frameworks that align national, regional, and local planning processes create coherence between development and sustainability goals. Mechanisms such as land zoning, environmental impact assessments, and strategic environmental planning can balance competing needs. Participatory land governance involving communities, private actors, and civil society ensures equitable decision-making and reduces social conflict over land rights.

Economic and financial mechanisms support strategic land management by internalizing the value of ecosystem services and encouraging sustainable practices. Payments for ecosystem services, land restoration funds, and carbon markets create incentives for maintaining forest and soil health. Conversely, reforming subsidies that encourage overexploitation of land and water resources reduces unsustainable practices. Linking economic valuation to land-use planning ensures that resource competition is managed based on true social and ecological costs rather than short-term economic gains.

Land-use change and resource competition are defining challenges of the WEFEC Nexus. Effective management depends on integrating ecological limits, economic realities, and social priorities into cohesive planning systems. Strategic land-use governance supports the balance between development and conservation, enabling societies to meet water, energy, and food demands while preserving ecosystem functions essential for long-term resilience.

Restoration and Nature-Based Solutions

Nature-based solutions are approaches that use ecosystems and natural processes to address environmental, social, and economic challenges. Within the WEFEC Nexus, they serve as integrative strategies that enhance resilience, restore ecological balance, and improve human well-being. By leveraging the inherent functions of nature—such as water filtration, carbon storage, and biodiversity maintenance—these solutions address multiple Nexus dimensions simultaneously, reducing vulnerability to climate change while supporting sustainable development.

Ecosystem restoration forms the cornerstone of nature-based solutions. Restoring degraded forests, wetlands, and grasslands revitalizes ecosystem services that underpin water, energy, and food systems. Forest restoration improves watershed regulation by enhancing infiltration, reducing erosion, and stabilizing flows during droughts and floods. Wetland restoration reestablishes natural water storage and purification functions, improving water quality and moderating flood risks. Grassland and mangrove restoration strengthen soil stability and sequester carbon, contributing to climate mitigation. These restoration activities also support biodiversity recovery, which enhances ecosystem adaptability under changing environmental conditions.

Reforestation and afforestation are key nature-based strategies that contribute to multiple Nexus objectives. Forest ecosystems regulate local and regional climates, conserve soil moisture, and maintain hydrological cycles essential for agriculture and energy production. Trees intercept rainfall, reducing runoff and enhancing groundwater recharge. They also serve as carbon sinks, storing atmospheric carbon dioxide in biomass and soils. Integrating trees into agricultural landscapes through agroforestry enhances productivity by improving soil fertility, providing shade, and stabilizing microclimates. Managed sustainably, forest landscapes provide renewable materials and energy sources without compromising ecosystem integrity.

Wetland restoration supports water security, biodiversity, and climate resilience. Wetlands act as natural filters, removing sediments, nutrients, and pollutants from water before it enters rivers and aquifers. They store floodwaters, reducing downstream flooding and replenishing groundwater reserves. In coastal regions, mangroves and salt marshes protect shorelines from storm surges and erosion, safeguarding infrastructure and livelihoods. Wetlands also serve as carbon sinks, capturing and storing significant amounts of organic carbon. Protecting and restoring wetlands therefore contributes to water quality improvement, disaster risk reduction, and climate mitigation simultaneously.

Soil and landscape restoration enhance the productivity and resilience of agricultural and ecological systems. Degraded soils lose their capacity to retain nutrients and water, reducing agricultural yields and increasing vulnerability to drought. Restoring soil organic matter through practices such as cover cropping, compost application, and reduced tillage rebuilds soil structure and fertility. These measures increase water infiltration and retention, reducing irrigation demand and energy use. Landscape-scale restoration— such as recontouring degraded slopes and stabilizing riverbanks— reduces erosion, enhances sediment balance, and improves ecosystem connectivity. Healthy soils and landscapes underpin sustainable food and water systems within the Nexus.

Urban ecosystems also benefit from nature-based approaches that enhance climate resilience and livability. Green roofs, urban forests, and permeable surfaces moderate temperatures, reduce runoff, and improve air quality. These systems complement gray infrastructure by managing stormwater naturally and enhancing biodiversity within urban areas. Urban wetlands and green corridors restore ecological connectivity and provide recreational spaces that improve mental health and community well-being. Incorporating nature-based designs into urban planning supports sustainable growth while reducing resource consumption and environmental stress.

Nature-based solutions also play a vital role in climate adaptation. As climate change intensifies floods, droughts, and temperature extremes, ecosystems that regulate water, carbon, and energy flows become essential buffers. Forests moderate heat and protect watersheds, wetlands absorb excess rainfall, and grasslands reduce dust and land degradation. Integrating these natural defenses into infrastructure and land-use planning reduces vulnerability while maintaining ecosystem services. Combined with renewable energy and efficient agricultural practices, nature-based adaptation strengthens the resilience of societies and economies to climate-related disruptions.

Economic and policy frameworks are essential to scaling nature-based solutions. Investments in ecosystem restoration generate long-term returns through reduced disaster costs, improved water and food security, and enhanced carbon sequestration. Economic instruments such as payment for ecosystem services, green bonds, and carbon markets can finance large-scale restoration efforts. Policymaking should integrate ecosystem considerations into water, energy, and agricultural strategies to ensure coherence across sectors. Cross-institutional coordination and community participation are also crucial for aligning local actions with national sustainability goals.

Monitoring and scientific assessment ensure that nature-based solutions remain effective and adaptive. Indicators such as biodiversity levels, soil organic carbon, and water retention capacity help measure ecological recovery. Spatial modeling tools can evaluate the trade-offs and co-benefits of restoration initiatives across the Nexus. Combining traditional ecological knowledge with modern science enhances project design and implementation. Transparent monitoring frameworks enable stakeholders to assess outcomes, adjust practices, and optimize resource allocation.

Nature-based solutions provide a systems-based pathway to address interlinked challenges of water scarcity, energy security, food production, and climate change. They align human development with natural processes, transforming degradation into regeneration. By embedding restoration and ecosystem-based management within the WEFEC Nexus, societies can build adaptive, resilient, and sustainable futures that balance environmental integrity with human prosperity.

Integrating Ecosystem Valuation into Policy

Integrating ecosystem valuation into policy connects ecological processes with economic and social systems, ensuring that the benefits provided by nature are recognized and accounted for in decision-making. The WEFEC Nexus depends on ecosystem services that support resource availability, climate regulation, and livelihood security. However, these benefits often remain unquantified, leading to policy and investment decisions that overlook their true value. Economic valuation provides a framework for assigning measurable worth to ecosystem services, enabling policymakers to internalize environmental externalities and design policies that balance development with sustainability.

Ecosystem valuation identifies and quantifies the benefits that ecosystems provide, including provisioning, regulating, supporting, and cultural services. Provisioning services—such as freshwater, timber, and food—are the most visible and easily monetized, while regulating services like carbon sequestration, flood control, and water purification often remain undervalued. Supporting services such as nutrient cycling and soil formation underpin all others but are challenging to express in market terms. Cultural services, including recreation, spiritual value, and heritage, contribute to well-being yet are rarely incorporated into formal policy assessments. Comprehensive valuation methods that account for both tangible and intangible services provide a more accurate representation of ecosystems' total economic contribution.

Valuation approaches can be grouped into market-based, revealed preference, and stated preference methods. Market-based valuation uses observed market prices for goods directly extracted from ecosystems. For example, timber and fish prices reflect provisioning services, while carbon credits can represent sequestration value. Revealed preference methods infer ecosystem value from related market behavior, such as travel cost models estimating recreational demand or hedonic pricing capturing how environmental quality affects property values. Stated preference methods, including contingent valuation and choice modeling, rely on surveys that elicit individuals' willingness to pay for ecosystem protection or restoration. Combining these methods allows for a more complete understanding of ecosystem values across diverse contexts and scales.

Integrating valuation into policy frameworks helps governments internalize environmental costs and benefits, transforming them from externalities into core economic considerations. Traditional policy and investment models often treat ecosystem degradation as a side effect rather than a measurable loss. By embedding valuation into cost-benefit analyses, policymakers can compare ecological and economic trade-offs explicitly. For instance, preserving wetlands may yield higher long-term returns through flood protection and water purification than converting them to agricultural use. Including ecosystem values in national accounting systems—such as through natural capital accounts—ensures that resource depletion and degradation are reflected in measures of economic performance, guiding more sustainable fiscal and development policies.

Valuation supports resource allocation by revealing the true costs and benefits of competing land, water, and energy uses. In the WEFEC Nexus, decisions about irrigation expansion, hydropower development, or land conversion often overlook downstream or long-term ecological impacts. Valuation allows decision-makers to identify where ecosystem services provide higher returns on investment than engineered alternatives. For example, watershed restoration may be more cost-effective than constructing water treatment facilities. By quantifying such benefits, governments can prioritize investments that deliver multiple Nexus outcomes—improving water quality, enhancing biodiversity, and sequestering carbon—within a single intervention.

Economic valuation also strengthens environmental governance by supporting regulatory and incentive-based instruments. Policies such as pollution taxes, PES, and tradable resource permits rely on accurate valuation data. PES schemes compensate landowners or communities for maintaining forests, wetlands, or grasslands that deliver ecosystem services such as water filtration or carbon storage. Valuation informs the design of these mechanisms by determining fair compensation rates and identifying priority areas for protection. Similarly, resource pricing reforms guided by valuation can eliminate subsidies that encourage overuse and degradation, aligning market signals with ecological sustainability.

Institutional integration of valuation requires coordination among economic, environmental, and social agencies. Ministries of finance, agriculture, energy, and environment must collaborate to incorporate ecosystem values into planning and budgeting processes. Establishing cross-sectoral frameworks ensures that ecosystem services are considered alongside infrastructure, trade, and industrial policies. This integration extends to international cooperation, where valuation supports compliance with global frameworks such as the SDGs, the Convention on Biological Diversity (CBD), and the Paris Agreement. Embedding valuation into climate finance mechanisms—such as carbon markets and green bonds—ensures that ecosystem services contribute directly to mitigation and adaptation objectives.

Valuation also enhances equity and inclusivity by recognizing the social and cultural dimensions of ecosystem benefits. Many rural and Indigenous communities depend on ecosystem services for subsistence, identity, and livelihoods. Incorporating their knowledge and values into valuation processes ensures that policy decisions respect cultural heritage and local priorities. Participatory valuation methods engage communities in assessing ecosystem benefits and trade-offs, fostering shared responsibility and stewardship. This inclusive approach supports environmental justice by ensuring that the costs and benefits of ecosystem management are distributed fairly across society.

Challenges to ecosystem valuation include data limitations, methodological uncertainty, and institutional resistance to non-market values. Ecological processes are complex and often non-linear, making it difficult to assign precise monetary values. Some ecosystem functions may have intrinsic or ethical importance that cannot be captured through economics alone. To address these limitations, policymakers can adopt a hybrid approach that combines quantitative valuation with qualitative assessment. This ensures that decision-making considers ecological thresholds, social values, and long-term sustainability rather than relying solely on financial metrics.

Integrating ecosystem valuation into policy strengthens the foundation of the WEFEC Nexus by aligning economic incentives with ecological resilience. It transforms the perception of ecosystems from passive backdrops to active contributors to national wealth and well-being. When ecosystem values are systematically included in governance, planning, and finance, societies can achieve more balanced and sustainable outcomes—protecting natural capital while advancing economic and social development.

Chapter 6: Climate Change as a Cross-Cutting Nexus Driver

Climate change intensifies the interdependencies across the WEFEC Nexus, influencing availability, quality, and stability of essential resources. Rising temperatures alter precipitation patterns, accelerate glacial melt, and increase evaporation, disrupting water supplies that underpin energy and food production. These shifts compound stress on ecosystems, reducing their capacity to regulate climate and maintain biodiversity. At the same time, mitigation and adaptation efforts within one sector can create ripple effects—both positive and negative—across others. Understanding climate change as a systemic driver within the Nexus enables coordinated strategies that enhance resilience, reduce vulnerabilities, and optimize resource co-management.

Climate Impacts on Resource Systems

Climate variability affects every component of the WEFEC Nexus, altering resource availability, system performance, and long-term sustainability. Changes in temperature, precipitation, and extreme weather patterns modify how resources interact, intensifying pressures across sectors. Integrated climate risk assessments help identify vulnerabilities, evaluate interdependencies, and inform adaptive planning that strengthens resilience within and between resource systems.

Water systems are among the most directly affected by climate change. Altered precipitation regimes influence river flows, groundwater recharge, and reservoir storage, leading to both scarcity and excess. Droughts reduce water supply for agriculture, industry, and households, while floods damage infrastructure and degrade water quality. Higher temperatures accelerate evaporation, concentrating pollutants and increasing demand for cooling in power generation. Glacial retreat and snowpack reduction disrupt seasonal water availability in regions dependent on meltwater. As climate patterns shift, water management systems must adapt to greater uncertainty, emphasizing flexible allocation, improved efficiency, and protection of ecosystem flows.

Energy systems face significant climate-related challenges through both supply and demand dynamics. Hydropower generation depends on stable water availability, making it vulnerable to changing rainfall and runoff patterns. Thermal power plants require large volumes of water for cooling, exposing them to risks during heatwaves and droughts. Renewable energy sources, while less water-dependent, are also influenced by climatic variability—solar output fluctuates with cloud cover, and wind generation is sensitive to changes in wind patterns. On the demand side, warmer temperatures increase energy needs for cooling while reducing heating demand in colder regions. Integrated planning between water and energy sectors ensures that energy transitions account for future hydrological and climatic variability, maintaining both reliability and sustainability.

Food systems are particularly sensitive to climatic conditions. Crop growth depends on predictable rainfall, moderate temperatures, and fertile soils—all factors increasingly disrupted by climate change. Higher temperatures shorten growing seasons and reduce yields for many staple crops, while extreme heat events damage livestock productivity. Shifting rainfall patterns can cause both drought stress and flood damage to agricultural land. Additionally, increased pest and disease outbreaks under warmer and more humid conditions further threaten food security. Adaptation measures such as improved irrigation efficiency, climate-resilient crop varieties, and diversified production systems reduce vulnerability and maintain stable food supply under changing climate regimes.

Ecosystems respond to climate change through shifts in species composition, productivity, and function. Warming temperatures alter habitat ranges, forcing species migration and threatening biodiversity. Coral reefs, wetlands, forests, and polar ecosystems face heightened risks due to temperature and moisture stress. These changes affect ecosystem services vital to human systems—such as water filtration, carbon sequestration, and soil stabilization—creating cascading effects throughout the Nexus. Degraded ecosystems lose their ability to buffer against climate extremes, amplifying risks to water, food, and energy systems. Maintaining ecosystem integrity through conservation, restoration, and adaptive management enhances the capacity of natural systems to mitigate and absorb climate shocks.

Climate impacts also intensify competition for land, water, and energy. Drought conditions heighten competition between agriculture and energy production, especially in water-scarce regions dependent on irrigation and cooling water. Declining hydropower capacity may increase reliance on fossil fuels, raising emissions and reinforcing climate feedbacks. Land conversion for bioenergy crops can displace food production and reduce biodiversity. These intersectoral pressures require coordinated responses that balance resource needs while minimizing trade-offs. Integrated governance frameworks and multi-sector planning tools can identify solutions that deliver co-benefits across the Nexus.

Extreme weather events represent some of the most immediate threats to resource systems. Floods, storms, and droughts disrupt infrastructure networks, cause economic losses, and displace communities. Damage to water and energy systems during such events leads to cascading failures that impact food production and public health. Building climate-resilient infrastructure—such as flood-resistant water systems, decentralized renewable energy, and adaptive agricultural practices—reduces systemic vulnerability. Risk management approaches that combine early warning systems, climate forecasting, and disaster preparedness help mitigate impacts and ensure continuity of essential services.

Climate change also affects the temporal and spatial distribution of resource availability. Regions once considered resource-abundant may face new constraints, while previously marginal areas may gain productivity. These shifts necessitate adaptive planning based on long-term projections and scenario modeling. Incorporating climate risk assessments into policy and investment decisions ensures that new infrastructure and land-use choices remain viable under a range of future conditions. Adaptive management approaches, supported by continuous monitoring and flexible governance, allow systems to adjust to evolving climatic realities.

Economic and social dimensions of climate impacts on resource systems must also be considered. Vulnerable populations, particularly in developing regions, often depend on climate-sensitive sectors such as agriculture and fisheries. Reduced productivity and resource availability can exacerbate poverty, migration, and inequality. Climate adaptation policies should integrate equity and inclusion, ensuring that adaptation benefits reach marginalized groups. Financial instruments such as climate insurance, risk-sharing mechanisms, and adaptive investment planning can reduce exposure and strengthen resilience at community and national levels.

Integrated climate risk assessments provide the analytical foundation for addressing these challenges. By mapping vulnerabilities across sectors, assessing interdependencies, and quantifying potential losses, policymakers can prioritize adaptation strategies that maximize co-benefits. Linking climate models with resource system analyses enables more accurate forecasting of future conditions and informs cross-sectoral coordination. Integrating these assessments into policy frameworks aligns adaptation planning with national development goals, ensuring that climate resilience is embedded in the long-term management of water, energy, food, and ecosystems.

Climate variability and change redefine how societies must manage their interconnected resource systems. Adaptive governance that integrates scientific evidence, economic valuation, and ecosystem-based approaches provides the most effective means to navigate this uncertainty. Through coordinated planning and resilient infrastructure, the WEFEC Nexus can transform climate risks into opportunities for sustainable, low-carbon, and inclusive development.

Mitigation through Nexus Synergies

Mitigation through Nexus synergies focuses on aligning climate actions across water, energy, food, and ecosystem systems to reduce greenhouse gas emissions while enhancing sustainability and resilience. Within the WEFEC Nexus, coordinated mitigation strategies recognize that each sector influences and depends on the others. When policies and technologies are designed to maximize co-benefits, they generate more efficient, equitable, and durable outcomes than isolated interventions. This integrated approach ensures that emission reduction measures contribute simultaneously to resource security, ecosystem protection, and economic stability.

Renewable energy adoption serves as a cornerstone of mitigation strategies that deliver multiple Nexus benefits. Transitioning from fossil fuels to low-carbon energy sources such as solar, wind, hydropower, and geothermal reduces greenhouse gas emissions and lessens air pollution, contributing to cleaner water and healthier ecosystems. Renewable energy systems also have lower water requirements than conventional thermal power generation, alleviating stress on freshwater resources. For instance, solar photovoltaic and wind technologies require negligible water for operation, freeing water for agricultural and ecological uses. Integrating renewable energy into irrigation systems, desalination plants, and wastewater treatment facilities further amplifies synergies by lowering emissions and enhancing water security.

Energy efficiency measures complement renewable deployment in achieving mitigation goals. Improving energy efficiency in agriculture, industry, and urban infrastructure reduces both emissions and operational costs. Efficient irrigation pumps, cold storage facilities, and food processing technologies minimize energy waste while safeguarding food supply chains. In the water sector, energy-efficient treatment and distribution systems lower emissions associated with pumping and purification. These measures extend beyond technological upgrades, encompassing behavioral and managerial practices such as optimized water scheduling and demand-side management. Enhanced efficiency across sectors ensures that mitigation efforts conserve resources while maintaining productivity and service reliability.

Sustainable agriculture represents another vital pathway for mitigation within the Nexus. Agricultural practices account for significant emissions from land-use change, fertilizers, and livestock. Transitioning toward low-emission, resource-efficient systems reduces the sector's climate footprint while strengthening resilience. Conservation tillage, precision nutrient management, and organic amendments improve soil health and enhance carbon sequestration. Agroforestry, integrating trees into farming systems, contributes to both mitigation and adaptation by capturing carbon, reducing erosion, and stabilizing microclimates. Sustainable livestock management—through improved feed efficiency, manure recycling, and rotational grazing—reduces methane emissions and promotes nutrient cycling. By aligning agricultural practices with climate goals, countries can achieve mitigation outcomes that also reinforce food security and ecosystem health.

Water management strategies provide another dimension of mitigation through Nexus synergies. Reducing non-revenue water losses, improving wastewater reuse, and optimizing hydropower operations lower both energy consumption and emissions. Treating and reusing wastewater decreases reliance on freshwater withdrawals while generating energy through biogas recovery. Natural infrastructure—such as wetlands and riparian buffers—filters pollutants and stores carbon, providing low-cost alternatives to engineered systems. Efficient water management enhances energy savings and promotes sustainable agricultural productivity, demonstrating how integrated approaches can yield broad climate and resource benefits.

Ecosystem conservation and restoration are essential components of Nexus-based mitigation. Healthy ecosystems function as carbon sinks, absorbing and storing atmospheric carbon dioxide in vegetation and soils. Protecting forests, mangroves, peatlands, and grasslands avoids emissions associated with land degradation and deforestation. Restoration activities enhance biodiversity, regulate hydrological cycles, and improve land productivity, generating co-benefits for water and food systems. Incorporating ecosystem-based mitigation into national climate strategies—such as through

reforestation, afforestation, and sustainable land-use planning—
aligns emission reduction with ecosystem resilience and human well-
being.

Integrated planning and governance mechanisms are critical to
realizing these synergies. Mitigation strategies often face trade-offs
between short-term economic gains and long-term sustainability. For
example, expanding biofuel production can reduce emissions from
fossil fuels but may compete with food production and water
availability. Coordinated governance frameworks help balance these
competing priorities by promoting cross-sectoral dialogue, shared
data systems, and joint policy development. Strategic environmental
assessments and integrated resource planning ensure that mitigation
measures in one sector do not inadvertently increase emissions or
pressures in another. Policymakers can use the Nexus framework to
identify and implement "no-regret" options—actions that yield
multiple benefits under a range of future conditions.

Financial and institutional innovations further enable the scaling of
Nexus-based mitigation. Green finance instruments, such as climate
bonds and carbon markets, channel investment toward projects that
deliver both emission reductions and resource efficiency.
International climate funds can prioritize integrated projects that link
renewable energy, sustainable agriculture, and ecosystem
restoration. Institutional coordination among ministries of energy,
water, and environment ensures that mitigation projects align with
national development goals. Transparent monitoring, reporting, and
verification systems track emission reductions while evaluating
broader resource impacts, improving accountability and policy
coherence.

Technological innovation and knowledge sharing accelerate progress
toward synergistic mitigation outcomes. Advances in digital
monitoring, remote sensing, and artificial intelligence enhance the
efficiency and precision of resource management. Data integration
across sectors enables predictive modeling of emissions and resource
flows, supporting evidence-based decision-making. Collaboration
between governments, research institutions, and private actors

fosters innovation and replication of best practices. Building capacity at the local level ensures that mitigation efforts are inclusive, context-specific, and sustainable over time.

Mitigation through Nexus synergies transforms climate action into a multidimensional opportunity. By aligning renewable energy expansion, sustainable agriculture, efficient water management, and ecosystem restoration, societies can achieve emission reductions while enhancing resilience and prosperity. Integrated approaches not only reduce climate risks but also strengthen the foundations of sustainable development, enabling a balanced transition toward low-carbon, resource-secure futures.

Adaptation Strategies within the Nexus

Adaptation strategies within the WEFEC Nexus focus on enhancing resilience and adaptive capacity across interconnected systems. As climate change intensifies variability in temperature, precipitation, and extreme events, integrated adaptation becomes critical to safeguard resources, ecosystems, and livelihoods. Nexus-based adaptation emphasizes coordination among sectors to minimize trade-offs and optimize co-benefits, ensuring that actions in one domain reinforce resilience in others. This approach prioritizes long-term sustainability by addressing the systemic nature of climate risks and leveraging synergies between water, energy, food, and ecosystems.

Water adaptation measures are foundational to building resilience across the Nexus. Climate change alters hydrological cycles, influencing both the quantity and quality of water resources. Expanding water storage through reservoirs, managed aquifer recharge, and natural retention systems helps stabilize supplies during droughts and floods. Decentralized water storage, such as farm ponds and urban rainwater harvesting, enhances local autonomy and reduces dependence on large-scale infrastructure. Improving irrigation efficiency through drip and sprinkler systems reduces water demand and energy use while maintaining agricultural productivity. Furthermore, integrating climate forecasts into water allocation planning allows adaptive management that responds dynamically to shifting rainfall and runoff patterns.

Diversifying agricultural systems enhances adaptive capacity and food security. Climate-resilient agriculture relies on crop diversification, soil conservation, and genetic improvements to reduce vulnerability to temperature and precipitation changes. Introducing drought-tolerant and heat-resistant crop varieties mitigates risks associated with shifting climate zones. Crop rotation and intercropping improve soil fertility and moisture retention, reducing dependence on external inputs. Diversifying production systems—combining crops, livestock, and aquaculture—spreads risk and enhances livelihood security. These measures, supported by early warning systems and climate-informed advisory services, enable farmers to make timely adjustments in planting and resource use, strengthening resilience at the local level.

Energy systems also require adaptation to ensure stability and reliability under changing climatic conditions. Renewable energy sources such as solar, wind, and hydropower are vulnerable to climate variability but also offer flexible opportunities for adaptation. Diversifying energy portfolios across multiple renewable sources enhances resilience by reducing dependence on single-resource systems. For example, hybrid renewable configurations—combining solar and wind generation—balance fluctuations in supply caused by weather changes. Energy storage technologies, including batteries and pumped hydro systems, stabilize energy availability during extreme events. Adaptation measures in the energy sector also include strengthening grid infrastructure against heatwaves, storms, and floods to ensure uninterrupted service for critical Nexus functions like water treatment and irrigation.

Ecosystems play a pivotal role in buffering climate impacts and sustaining adaptive capacity across sectors. Maintaining healthy forests, wetlands, and watersheds stabilizes water flows, prevents erosion, and moderates local climates. Green infrastructure—such as urban parks, green roofs, and permeable surfaces—reduces heat stress, manages stormwater, and enhances urban resilience. Protecting riparian zones and restoring degraded landscapes improve water retention and quality while providing habitat connectivity. Ecosystem-based adaptation integrates these natural systems into broader planning frameworks, ensuring that adaptation actions also support biodiversity and ecosystem services that underpin the WEFEC Nexus.

Institutional and governance frameworks are essential for implementing Nexus-based adaptation strategies effectively. Fragmented decision-making can undermine cross-sectoral coordination, leading to inefficient or conflicting responses. Strengthening policy coherence across ministries and levels of government ensures that adaptation efforts in one sector complement those in others. Integrated planning tools—such as climate-resilient infrastructure assessments and scenario modeling—help identify priorities and align investments. Establishing multi-stakeholder platforms encourages collaboration between public agencies, private actors, and local communities. This participatory approach fosters shared ownership and enhances social learning, allowing adaptation measures to evolve as climate risks and knowledge change.

Technological innovation supports adaptive capacity by improving resource efficiency and monitoring. Remote sensing, climate data analytics, and digital modeling enhance understanding of vulnerabilities and inform adaptive decision-making. Precision agriculture technologies optimize input use based on real-time environmental data, reducing resource waste and improving yield stability. Smart water systems use sensors and automation to detect leaks, monitor quality, and adjust delivery under variable conditions. In the energy sector, digital management platforms enable flexible demand response during periods of stress. Such innovations provide the analytical foundation for adaptive governance and operational flexibility across Nexus sectors.

Financial mechanisms enable the implementation and scaling of adaptation strategies. Climate finance instruments, such as adaptation funds and resilience bonds, support projects that deliver cross-sectoral benefits. Public–private partnerships mobilize investment in climate-resilient infrastructure, renewable energy, and sustainable agriculture. Insurance mechanisms—such as index-based crop or water insurance—reduce financial risks and promote recovery following extreme events. Integrating adaptation objectives into national budgets and development plans ensures long-term funding stability and policy continuity. Aligning these financial frameworks with Nexus priorities ensures that adaptation investments generate broad systemic resilience rather than isolated benefits.

Capacity building and knowledge sharing underpin effective adaptation. Local communities, technical experts, and policymakers require access to training, information, and decision-support tools tailored to specific contexts. Empowering local actors through participatory planning and education enhances adaptive behavior and ownership of interventions. Collaborative research networks foster innovation and facilitate the transfer of best practices across regions. Incorporating traditional and indigenous knowledge strengthens adaptive management by blending experiential understanding with modern science.

Adaptation strategies within the Nexus transform fragmented responses into integrated systems of resilience. Through coordinated water management, diversified agriculture, robust energy systems, and healthy ecosystems, societies can withstand and recover from climate stresses more effectively. These measures ensure that adaptation not only reduces vulnerability but also supports long-term sustainability, equity, and stability across the interconnected domains of water, energy, food, and ecosystems.

Policy Coherence and Global Commitments

Policy coherence and global commitments are essential for advancing the WEFEC Nexus as a framework for sustainable development. The interlinked nature of global environmental challenges demands coordination among policies addressing climate change, biodiversity, water management, and food security. Without alignment, fragmented policies risk creating inefficiencies, duplications, and unintended trade-offs that undermine sustainability objectives. Achieving coherence across governance levels—from local to international—ensures that adaptation, mitigation, and development policies reinforce one another within a unified vision of resilience and resource efficiency.

Policy coherence begins at the national level, where governments must harmonize sectoral strategies under integrated frameworks. Ministries responsible for energy, water, agriculture, and environment often pursue objectives independently, leading to competing priorities and inconsistent regulations. Aligning these policies requires institutional coordination mechanisms that bridge sectoral silos. National sustainable development strategies can serve as overarching frameworks for coherence, setting shared goals and indicators aligned with the WEFEC Nexus. Integrating cross-sectoral planning tools such as strategic environmental assessments (SEAs) and integrated resource management frameworks ensures that policies in one sector consider impacts and dependencies in others. This approach not only improves efficiency but also strengthens resilience to climate and resource-related shocks.

At the global level, multiple international agreements shape the governance landscape of the Nexus. The 2030 Agenda for Sustainable Development provides a unifying framework through the SDGs, which embody the interconnectedness of water (SDG 6), energy (SDG 7), food (SDG 2), ecosystems (SDG 15), and climate (SDG 13). Achieving these goals requires integrated implementation that recognizes synergies and trade-offs among them. The Paris Agreement on climate change complements the SDGs by promoting low-carbon transitions and climate resilience, both of which depend on sustainable resource management. Similarly, the Convention on Biological Diversity (CBD) underscores ecosystem health as foundational to human well-being and economic stability. Aligning national commitments under these frameworks creates policy coherence across the global sustainability agenda.

81

Coherence among global agreements is reinforced through institutional linkages and reporting mechanisms. Countries are increasingly integrating Nationally Determined Contributions (NDCs), National Biodiversity Strategies and Action Plans (NBSAPs), and National Adaptation Plans (NAPs) to avoid duplication and enhance synergies. For example, incorporating land-use and water management considerations into climate mitigation strategies ensures that emission reduction efforts also support biodiversity conservation and food security. The integration of Nexus principles into national reporting frameworks encourages governments to identify co-benefits and monitor progress holistically. This not only improves policy efficiency but also enhances transparency and accountability within the global governance system.

Regional cooperation further strengthens policy coherence by addressing shared resources and transboundary challenges. River basins, aquifers, and ecosystems often span national borders, requiring joint governance structures that balance diverse interests. Regional frameworks—such as those developed by the African Union, the European Union, and the Association of Southeast Asian Nations—promote cross-border coordination of energy grids, water management, and food systems. These cooperative arrangements align national policies with broader regional objectives, fostering resilience through shared infrastructure and collective adaptation strategies. In regions highly vulnerable to climate change, coordinated adaptation planning ensures that actions in one country do not exacerbate vulnerabilities in another.

Policy coherence also depends on the integration of scientific knowledge and data systems. Evidence-based policymaking enables decision-makers to identify interactions among sectors and evaluate potential outcomes of alternative policy choices. Developing shared data platforms and decision-support tools enhances transparency and facilitates collaboration among institutions. Integrated modeling frameworks, such as water-energy-food system models, support scenario analysis and policy simulation. These tools help policymakers anticipate long-term implications of decisions, balance competing demands, and allocate resources efficiently. Strengthening national statistical capacities and promoting data sharing among ministries and international organizations are vital for achieving consistency and coherence across governance levels.

Financing mechanisms play a pivotal role in operationalizing coherent Nexus-based policies. Global climate funds, development banks, and bilateral donors increasingly recognize the need for integrated investments that deliver multiple sustainability outcomes. Aligning financial flows with Nexus objectives ensures that adaptation, mitigation, and development initiatives are mutually reinforcing. For instance, projects that combine renewable energy generation, sustainable agriculture, and ecosystem restoration deliver broader benefits than isolated interventions. Integrating Nexus considerations into financing criteria and project evaluation processes encourages cross-sectoral collaboration and innovation. Coherent financing frameworks also help avoid policy contradictions, such as subsidies that support fossil fuel use or water-intensive agriculture.

Effective governance structures must balance top-down coordination with bottom-up engagement. Policy coherence is strengthened when local actors, civil society, and the private sector participate in decision-making. Local governments play a crucial role in implementing global and national commitments, translating abstract goals into practical actions. Inclusive governance ensures that adaptation and mitigation strategies reflect diverse social, cultural, and ecological contexts. Participatory approaches also enhance legitimacy and compliance by fostering ownership among stakeholders. Building institutional capacity at all levels—through training, information exchange, and resource support—enables effective coordination and implementation of coherent policies.

Monitoring and evaluation frameworks are essential for maintaining coherence over time. Establishing cross-sectoral indicators and performance metrics enables policymakers to track interlinkages and measure progress toward integrated objectives. These frameworks should capture not only economic and environmental outcomes but also social equity and governance effectiveness. Periodic policy reviews and feedback mechanisms facilitate adaptive management, allowing governments to adjust strategies in response to new knowledge, technologies, and climate realities. Transparent reporting enhances accountability and reinforces trust among stakeholders, sustaining long-term policy alignment.

Global coherence within the WEFEC Nexus ultimately requires political commitment and leadership. Governments must embrace systemic thinking, recognizing that sustainable development depends on interconnected resource systems. International cooperation, underpinned by shared values of equity and stewardship, provides the foundation for coordinated action. Embedding the Nexus approach in global governance frameworks ensures that adaptation, mitigation, and development policies converge toward common goals—promoting resilience, sustainability, and prosperity for present and future generations.

Chapter 7: Governance and Policy Integration

Governance and policy integration provide the institutional framework for implementing the WEFEC Nexus. Effective governance links fragmented sectors, aligning water, energy, agriculture, and environmental policies toward shared sustainability goals. By coordinating across ministries and administrative levels, Nexus-based governance ensures coherent strategies that balance resource use and environmental protection. Integrated policymaking also supports transparency, accountability, and long-term resilience.

Institutional Frameworks for Nexus Implementation

Effective governance of the WEFEC Nexus depends on institutional arrangements that foster collaboration, coordination, and coherence across sectors and scales. The interconnected nature of resource systems requires frameworks capable of managing interdependencies, mediating trade-offs, and ensuring equitable access to resources. Institutional frameworks thus serve as the backbone for operationalizing Nexus principles, translating integrated concepts into actionable policy and practice.

Institutional design determines how responsibilities are distributed among government ministries, agencies, and local authorities. Historically, water, energy, and agricultural sectors have evolved within separate governance domains, leading to fragmented decision-making. This siloed structure hinders the implementation of integrated approaches. Effective Nexus governance calls for cross-sectoral coordination through inter-ministerial committees, joint planning bodies, and integrated resource management authorities. Such arrangements facilitate dialogue among institutions with overlapping mandates, enabling coherent policy formulation and synchronized investment planning. The creation of centralized coordination mechanisms ensures that decisions in one sector—such as energy policy—do not undermine progress in others, like water conservation or food security.

Decentralization adds another layer of complexity to institutional integration. Local governments often play a crucial role in implementing resource management policies but may lack the authority or capacity to coordinate across sectors. Strengthening multi-level governance frameworks bridges this gap by aligning national strategies with regional and local priorities. Establishing clear communication channels between central and local institutions ensures consistency in policy application while allowing flexibility to address regional contexts. Capacity building, financial support, and knowledge transfer enhance the ability of local authorities to operationalize Nexus principles effectively.

Legal and regulatory frameworks provide the foundation for institutional coordination. Laws governing water allocation, energy production, land use, and environmental protection must be harmonized to reduce conflicts and inefficiencies. Regulatory coherence can be achieved by embedding Nexus objectives into existing legislation or through new frameworks that explicitly promote cross-sectoral integration. For example, water laws can include provisions for energy efficiency in irrigation systems, while energy regulations can incentivize renewable projects with low water footprints. Legal mechanisms that promote transparency, accountability, and stakeholder participation strengthen institutional legitimacy and encourage shared responsibility for sustainable resource management.

Institutional collaboration extends beyond the public sector to include private enterprises, civil society, and academia. Multi-stakeholder platforms create spaces for dialogue and innovation, aligning diverse interests toward shared sustainability goals. Public-private partnerships (PPPs) can drive investment in Nexus-aligned infrastructure, such as renewable energy-powered desalination or wastewater reuse systems. Civil society organizations contribute by advocating for equitable access and environmental protection, while academic and research institutions provide data, modeling tools, and policy analysis to support evidence-based decision-making. Integrating these actors into formal institutional frameworks enhances the adaptive capacity and resilience of Nexus governance systems.

International and regional organizations play a complementary role by providing guidance, technical assistance, and financial support for Nexus implementation. Many countries rely on external frameworks—such as the United Nations' SDGs, the Paris Agreement, and the Convention on Biological Diversity (CBD)—to shape national governance structures. Donor agencies and multilateral development banks increasingly prioritize integrated approaches in funding criteria, encouraging institutional reforms that promote Nexus coherence. Cross-border cooperation mechanisms, particularly for shared water and energy resources, further enhance institutional alignment. River basin organizations and regional councils exemplify cooperative governance structures that integrate multiple sectors and stakeholders.

Data management and information sharing are critical enablers of institutional integration. Fragmented data systems across ministries hinder comprehensive analysis and joint planning. Establishing shared information platforms supports transparency and coordination by allowing institutions to access consistent datasets on water use, energy demand, land cover, and ecosystem conditions. Integrated modeling tools and geospatial databases enable policymakers to assess interlinkages, forecast trade-offs, and evaluate the impacts of policy options. Institutional mandates should include mechanisms for regular data exchange, standardized reporting, and joint monitoring of progress toward Nexus objectives.

Institutional performance also depends on financial and human resources. Implementing Nexus-based governance requires investment in intersectoral coordination mechanisms, technical training, and policy innovation. Dedicated funding streams for integrated projects—supported by climate finance, development assistance, or national budgets—can bridge institutional divides. Building human capacity through training programs, workshops, and academic curricula ensures that policymakers, planners, and practitioners possess the interdisciplinary skills necessary for Nexus implementation. Incentive structures that reward collaboration and innovation encourage institutional actors to adopt integrated approaches in practice.

Accountability mechanisms reinforce the effectiveness of institutional frameworks. Clear delineation of roles and responsibilities minimizes overlap and promotes efficiency. Performance indicators linked to Nexus objectives help track institutional contributions to sustainable resource management. Periodic audits, policy evaluations, and stakeholder feedback mechanisms provide opportunities for continuous improvement. Transparent reporting fosters trust among institutions and stakeholders, enhancing legitimacy and compliance with Nexus principles.

Institutional adaptability is essential to respond to emerging challenges such as climate change, demographic shifts, and technological innovation. Governance structures must evolve to integrate new information, respond to crises, and accommodate shifts in policy priorities. Adaptive governance frameworks emphasize flexibility, learning, and iterative decision-making. Establishing feedback loops between policy design and implementation allows institutions to refine strategies in light of observed outcomes. This dynamic approach ensures that institutional frameworks remain relevant and effective amid changing environmental and socioeconomic conditions.

Ultimately, effective Nexus implementation relies on institutions that transcend traditional boundaries to embrace interconnectedness as a guiding principle. Building coordination across sectors, scales, and stakeholders transforms governance from reactive management to proactive stewardship of shared resources. Institutional frameworks that embody inclusivity, transparency, and adaptability provide the foundation for sustainable, resilient, and equitable resource systems within the WEFEC Nexus.

Legal and Regulatory Instruments

Laws and regulations define how natural resources are governed, allocated, and utilized across sectors. They provide the foundation for ensuring that the use of water, energy, land, and ecosystems aligns with sustainability objectives. However, many existing frameworks were designed within sectoral boundaries and are ill-equipped to address interdependencies across systems. Reforming these legal structures to promote integration and coordination is essential for achieving effective governance under the WEFEC Nexus.

Legal instruments influence the rights, responsibilities, and incentives that guide resource use. Water laws determine allocation priorities among agriculture, industry, and domestic sectors, while energy legislation shapes production and consumption patterns. Agricultural policies influence land use and irrigation demand, and environmental laws regulate pollution and conservation. In many countries, these sector-specific laws function independently, resulting in overlapping mandates, conflicting objectives, and administrative inefficiencies. Aligning legal instruments ensures that one sector's regulatory framework does not undermine sustainability goals in another.

Integrating Nexus principles into law begins with establishing legal recognition of interconnections among resources. Framework legislation can explicitly reference cross-sectoral dependencies, mandating coordination across ministries and agencies. For example, water laws can incorporate energy efficiency requirements for irrigation systems or require environmental impact assessments that include downstream effects on ecosystems and food production. Similarly, energy legislation can include provisions on water use efficiency for thermal power generation or incentives for renewable energy projects that reduce water demand. These cross-cutting legal provisions institutionalize Nexus thinking within regulatory structures.

Regulatory coherence can be strengthened through harmonization and modernization of existing frameworks. Outdated or conflicting laws can be revised to align with sustainability objectives and contemporary challenges such as climate change, population growth, and technological change. Codifying integrated resource management principles within sectoral laws ensures consistency across governance levels. For instance, national environmental laws can include specific clauses mandating the integration of ecosystem services valuation in water and land management decisions. The development of overarching natural resource management laws can unify fragmented statutes under a single framework, promoting efficiency and coordination.

Legal instruments also establish mechanisms for stakeholder participation and transparency in resource governance. Inclusive processes ensure that affected communities, private actors, and civil society organizations have opportunities to contribute to policy formulation and implementation. Participatory rights enshrined in law enhance legitimacy and accountability, fostering shared ownership of resource management outcomes. Public access to environmental information and consultation processes mandated by law, such as environmental impact assessment hearings, support transparency and informed decision-making.

Regulatory tools such as permits, standards, and quotas operationalize Nexus-based governance. Licensing systems for water abstraction, energy production, and land conversion can be designed to reflect resource interdependencies. For example, water abstraction permits can require compliance with efficiency standards, while energy generation licenses can incorporate limits on water use intensity. Emission standards and effluent discharge limits protect ecosystem functions by reducing pollution pressures on water and soil resources. Quotas for groundwater extraction or agricultural expansion help prevent overexploitation and maintain balance across interconnected systems.

Economic instruments complement regulatory measures by providing financial incentives or disincentives aligned with sustainability objectives. Legal frameworks can authorize taxes, subsidies, and market-based mechanisms that encourage resource efficiency and conservation. Water pricing policies can promote efficient use by reflecting scarcity values, while feed-in tariffs and renewable energy credits can accelerate the transition to low-water, low-carbon energy systems. Payments for ecosystem services (PES) programs, formalized under law, reward landowners or communities for maintaining forested watersheds or wetlands that deliver multiple Nexus benefits. Integrating such instruments within legal frameworks ensures long-term institutional stability and equitable implementation.

Legal reforms must also consider equity and access to resources. Laws that define property rights, land tenure, and water access determine who benefits from resource use and who bears environmental costs. Clarifying and securing rights for marginalized groups, including women, Indigenous peoples, and smallholder farmers, promotes social inclusion and enhances resilience. Integrating equity principles into legal frameworks ensures that resource management supports both environmental and social sustainability.

Enforcement mechanisms are essential for the effectiveness of legal and regulatory instruments. Weak enforcement undermines compliance and perpetuates unsustainable practices. Strengthening monitoring, inspection, and sanctioning procedures ensures that laws are implemented as intended. Establishing specialized environmental courts or tribunals can improve the resolution of disputes related to resource use and environmental harm. Legal provisions for adaptive management allow for periodic review and revision of regulations based on evolving scientific knowledge and environmental conditions.

At the international level, treaties and conventions establish shared legal obligations for managing transboundary resources and addressing global challenges. Instruments such as the Paris Agreement, the Convention on Biological Diversity, and the Ramsar Convention on Wetlands guide national legislation toward sustainability objectives. Regional agreements on shared river basins or aquifers provide frameworks for cooperative management among neighboring states. Aligning national legal systems with international commitments enhances policy coherence and fosters collective progress toward sustainable resource governance.

Reforming and aligning legal and regulatory frameworks to reflect Nexus principles strengthens governance capacity and fosters resilience. Integrated legal instruments provide a foundation for managing interconnected resources sustainably, ensuring that economic development proceeds without compromising environmental integrity or social equity.

Cross-Sectoral Planning and Decision Tools

Cross-sectoral planning and decision tools provide the analytical foundation for implementing the WEFEC Nexus. These tools help policymakers and planners understand complex interactions, evaluate trade-offs, and identify synergies across sectors. By integrating data, models, and scenarios, they support the design of coherent strategies that balance competing objectives and ensure sustainable resource management.

Integrated assessment models (IAMs) are central to Nexus planning. They combine information from multiple disciplines—such as hydrology, energy systems, agriculture, and economics—into a single analytical framework. IAMs allow users to explore how policy decisions or external drivers affect multiple sectors simultaneously. For example, an IAM can assess how water scarcity constrains energy generation or how bioenergy expansion influences land and food security. These models often include feedback loops and scenario analysis capabilities, enabling evaluation of long-term sustainability pathways under different policy or climate conditions.

System dynamics modeling complements integrated assessments by emphasizing feedback mechanisms and time-dependent processes. This approach uses causal loops and stock-flow structures to simulate the behavior of interconnected systems over time. Policymakers can visualize how interventions in one sector ripple through others, revealing unintended consequences and identifying leverage points for intervention. System dynamics is particularly useful for testing policy options before implementation, helping avoid costly or counterproductive measures. Through iterative modeling, stakeholders can refine strategies based on emerging data and evolving priorities.

Spatially explicit models, including geographic information systems (GIS), enhance the understanding of Nexus interlinkages at regional and local scales. GIS tools map resource availability, infrastructure, and environmental conditions, providing a visual basis for decision-making. Overlaying data on water basins, energy grids, agricultural zones, and ecosystems allows policymakers to identify areas of potential conflict or synergy. Spatial modeling supports land-use planning, resource allocation, and risk assessment by revealing geographic dependencies and hotspots of vulnerability. Coupled with remote sensing data, GIS enhances monitoring capabilities and enables dynamic updates to resource management plans.

Multi-criteria decision analysis (MCDA) provides a structured framework for comparing alternative policies or projects based on multiple objectives. It allows stakeholders to evaluate options that may not be directly comparable in economic terms, such as trade-offs between energy efficiency and ecosystem preservation. MCDA incorporates quantitative and qualitative criteria, reflecting social, environmental, and economic considerations. This inclusive approach ensures that decision-making captures diverse stakeholder perspectives, balancing short-term development goals with long-term sustainability outcomes.

Scenario analysis and foresight methods extend cross-sectoral planning into the future by exploring possible trajectories under different assumptions. Scenarios help decision-makers prepare for uncertainty by examining how trends in population growth, technological change, or climate conditions could alter resource demand and availability. Foresight exercises engage policymakers, scientists, and stakeholders in co-developing narratives about desirable and plausible futures. These narratives guide strategic planning and policy formulation, fostering resilience and adaptability in governance systems.

Economic and environmental accounting frameworks, such as natural capital accounting and input-output models, integrate Nexus perspectives into macroeconomic planning. These tools quantify the interdependencies among sectors in terms of material and energy flows, emissions, and ecosystem services. By linking environmental indicators to economic performance, they inform decisions on investments, subsidies, and resource pricing. Governments can use these frameworks to identify inefficiencies, design fiscal instruments, and measure progress toward sustainable development targets. Incorporating natural capital into national accounts ensures that environmental assets are recognized as integral components of economic wealth.

Participatory modeling and decision-support systems enhance collaboration across institutions and stakeholders. These tools combine scientific analysis with stakeholder input to co-create shared understanding and consensus around policy choices. Participatory approaches build trust, align priorities, and improve the legitimacy of decisions. Decision-support platforms that integrate data visualization, simulation, and user interaction enable continuous dialogue between policymakers, researchers, and practitioners. They help bridge the gap between technical analysis and practical implementation, ensuring that Nexus-informed policies are grounded in local realities.

Digital transformation expands the potential of Nexus decision tools through advanced analytics, big data, and artificial intelligence. Machine learning algorithms can process vast datasets to identify patterns, predict system behavior, and optimize resource allocation. Real-time monitoring systems, enabled by the Internet of Things (IoT), provide continuous data on water flows, energy consumption, and agricultural productivity. Linking these technologies through integrated platforms allows for adaptive management and rapid response to emerging challenges. Digital tools thus enhance precision, efficiency, and scalability in Nexus planning.

Capacity building is necessary for effective use of these analytical tools. Policymakers and practitioners must understand model assumptions, limitations, and appropriate applications to interpret results accurately. Training programs and collaborative research initiatives build technical skills and promote cross-sectoral literacy. Institutionalizing the use of integrated tools within planning agencies ensures continuity and consistency in applying the Nexus approach. Collaboration between academia, government, and the private sector accelerates tool development and fosters innovation in resource management.

Cross-sectoral planning and decision tools create a shared evidence base for integrated governance. By combining quantitative analysis, spatial data, and stakeholder input, they provide a foundation for coherent strategies that reflect the interconnected realities of resource systems. These tools enable decision-makers to anticipate trade-offs, identify synergies, and pursue policies that balance economic growth, environmental integrity, and social well-being.

Stakeholder Engagement and Participation

Stakeholder engagement and participation are central to effective governance within the WEFEC Nexus. Inclusive approaches ensure that communities, private sectors, and civil society contribute to the design, implementation, and monitoring of sustainable resource policies. By incorporating diverse perspectives, stakeholder participation strengthens transparency, legitimacy, and equity in decision-making, enabling governance systems to respond to complex interdependencies across sectors.

Engagement begins with identifying stakeholders who are directly or indirectly affected by resource management decisions. These include government institutions, private companies, non-governmental organizations, academia, local communities, and Indigenous groups. Each actor brings unique interests, capacities, and forms of knowledge that influence how resources are valued and managed. Mapping stakeholder relationships helps reveal power dynamics and potential conflicts of interest, providing a foundation for balanced representation. Ensuring that marginalized voices are included in consultations enhances fairness and social acceptance of policies.

Public participation mechanisms institutionalize inclusion by providing formal avenues for stakeholder input. These mechanisms may take the form of consultative forums, participatory planning workshops, or advisory councils. Legal frameworks often mandate such processes for environmental assessments, policy formulation, or infrastructure development. Transparent procedures for information sharing and feedback promote accountability and build trust between decision-makers and stakeholders. Access to timely and reliable data empowers participants to engage meaningfully in discussions and influence outcomes.

Incorporating local and Indigenous knowledge enhances the relevance and resilience of Nexus governance. Communities living within resource landscapes often possess deep understanding of ecological cycles, traditional management practices, and social norms that govern resource use. Integrating this knowledge with scientific data creates a more comprehensive basis for decision-making. Participatory approaches that respect customary rights and practices strengthen social cohesion and foster stewardship of natural resources. Collaborative frameworks between government institutions and community organizations facilitate joint monitoring, adaptive management, and conflict resolution.

Private sector participation plays a critical role in advancing sustainable resource management. Businesses in water-intensive, energy-producing, or agricultural sectors have significant influence over resource flows and environmental outcomes. Engaging the private sector in Nexus governance aligns corporate strategies with national sustainability objectives. Voluntary initiatives such as corporate water stewardship programs, renewable energy commitments, and sustainable sourcing standards contribute to reducing resource pressures. PPPs can leverage financial resources and technical expertise for integrated projects that deliver shared benefits across sectors.

Civil society organizations act as intermediaries between communities, governments, and private actors. They advocate for social equity, environmental protection, and transparency in policy processes. Their participation ensures that decision-making remains accountable to public interests. Civil society also contributes to capacity building through awareness campaigns, training programs, and technical assistance, empowering communities to engage effectively in Nexus-related initiatives. Collaborative platforms that connect civil society with policymakers create opportunities for co-production of solutions tailored to local conditions.

Stakeholder engagement extends to multi-level governance structures. Local participation supports context-specific solutions, while national and regional coordination ensures coherence with broader development goals. Cross-scale collaboration allows stakeholders to address issues that transcend administrative boundaries, such as transboundary water management or regional energy integration. Strengthening communication channels among governance levels facilitates knowledge exchange and harmonization of objectives. This interconnected structure enhances institutional capacity for managing shared resources efficiently and equitably.

Effective participation requires capacity development among stakeholders. Not all actors possess equal technical knowledge or negotiation skills to engage in complex policy discussions. Building capacity through training, education, and access to information reduces disparities and promotes informed dialogue. Governments and development partners can provide platforms for skill development, particularly for local communities and small organizations. Capacity building also extends to government agencies, ensuring that officials understand participatory methods and value stakeholder contributions as integral to policy design.

Engagement processes must be designed to ensure inclusivity, transparency, and continuity. Token participation—where stakeholders are consulted without genuine influence—undermines trust and weakens outcomes. Effective engagement requires clear objectives, structured dialogue, and feedback mechanisms that demonstrate how stakeholder input informs decisions. Long-term participation is sustained through institutionalized frameworks that extend beyond individual projects or policy cycles. Embedding engagement principles into governance structures creates stability and consistency in collaborative resource management.

Monitoring and evaluation mechanisms enable assessment of participation effectiveness. Indicators such as representation diversity, participation frequency, and responsiveness to stakeholder input measure the inclusiveness and quality of engagement processes. Independent reviews and public reporting enhance accountability and encourage continuous improvement. Learning from past experiences allows institutions to refine engagement strategies and adapt to evolving social and environmental contexts.

Stakeholder engagement and participation ensure that governance under the WEFEC Nexus reflects collective priorities and shared responsibility. Inclusive and transparent decision-making fosters cooperation among diverse actors, aligning social, economic, and environmental objectives through collaborative and adaptive governance.

Chapter 8: Technology and Innovation for Nexus Solutions

Technology and innovation drive the transformation of the WEFEC Nexus by enabling smarter, more efficient resource management. Advances in artificial intelligence, the Internet of Things, and remote sensing allow real-time monitoring and data integration across sectors. These tools enhance decision-making, optimize efficiency, and support predictive management of interconnected systems. Clean technologies, renewable energy, and circular resource innovations reduce pressures on water and land while lowering emissions. Integrating digital solutions and sustainable technologies across the Nexus strengthens resilience, improves coordination, and accelerates progress toward global sustainability and climate goals.

Digitalization and Smart Systems

Digitalization and smart systems are transforming how societies manage interconnected water, energy, food, ecosystem, and climate systems. The integration of artificial intelligence (AI), the IoT, and remote sensing technologies provides real-time data that enhances monitoring, analysis, and decision-making. These technologies enable more efficient use of resources, early detection of risks, and adaptive management strategies that strengthen resilience across the WEFEC Nexus.

Artificial intelligence contributes to Nexus governance by processing large volumes of complex data to identify patterns, optimize operations, and forecast system behaviors. Machine learning algorithms can analyze historical and real-time datasets to predict water demand, energy consumption, and crop yields. Predictive analytics support proactive management by anticipating shortages, equipment failures, or environmental stress. In water management, AI applications optimize reservoir operations, detect leaks in distribution systems, and improve demand forecasting. In agriculture, AI models analyze soil health, crop performance, and weather conditions to guide precision farming practices that minimize resource inputs while maintaining productivity.

The Internet of Things connects devices and sensors across infrastructure systems, providing continuous streams of operational data. IoT applications in water networks monitor flow rates, pressure levels, and quality indicators, allowing for real-time responses to anomalies. In energy systems, smart meters and sensors track generation, distribution, and consumption patterns, enhancing efficiency and supporting demand-side management. Agricultural IoT systems integrate soil moisture sensors, automated irrigation controls, and weather stations to optimize water and fertilizer use. By linking these devices through centralized platforms, decision-makers gain visibility into system performance and can respond quickly to disruptions or inefficiencies.

Remote sensing technologies offer a large-scale perspective on environmental conditions that complements ground-based data collection. Satellite imagery and aerial surveys provide valuable information on land cover, vegetation health, and water availability. These tools support the monitoring of ecosystem services, agricultural productivity, and climate impacts. For instance, remote sensing data can detect drought stress, map changes in water bodies, and track deforestation rates. Advances in sensor resolution and data processing have made remote sensing more accessible and accurate, enabling its integration into routine planning and monitoring frameworks.

Data integration and interoperability are essential for leveraging digital technologies within the Nexus. Multiple sectors generate vast but often fragmented datasets that are stored in incompatible formats. Developing interoperable data platforms allows for seamless exchange and analysis across systems. Cloud computing facilitates the storage and processing of large datasets, enabling real-time data sharing among institutions. Integrated platforms that combine data from water utilities, power grids, agricultural systems, and environmental sensors support holistic decision-making and coordination. Ensuring data standardization and interoperability strengthens the reliability and efficiency of cross-sectoral management.

Digital twins represent an emerging innovation in resource management. These virtual replicas of physical systems use real-time data to simulate performance, test scenarios, and evaluate policy interventions. In the WEFEC Nexus, digital twins can model interactions among water, energy, and agricultural systems, helping planners assess the implications of infrastructure investments or policy changes. For example, a digital twin of a river basin can simulate the impacts of hydropower operations on irrigation, ecosystem flows, and downstream communities. Decision-makers can test alternative strategies under varying climate and demand conditions, identifying options that optimize efficiency and minimize risk.

Blockchain technology enhances transparency and accountability in resource governance. Its distributed ledger system securely records transactions and data exchanges, reducing the risk of manipulation or error. In water management, blockchain can verify data from sensors or track water rights and allocation agreements. In energy systems, it can facilitate decentralized renewable energy trading among producers and consumers. Blockchain applications in agriculture support supply chain traceability, ensuring that production practices meet sustainability standards. Integrating blockchain into Nexus governance fosters trust among stakeholders and strengthens data integrity across sectors.

Digitalization also supports policy and regulatory innovation. Data-driven governance enables authorities to design adaptive and responsive regulatory frameworks. Real-time monitoring facilitates enforcement of environmental standards and water quality regulations. Automated reporting systems reduce administrative burdens and improve compliance. Digital tools enhance transparency by providing public access to environmental data, enabling citizens and civil society organizations to hold institutions accountable. Policymakers can use digital dashboards to visualize performance indicators and track progress toward national sustainability targets.

The deployment of digital technologies requires robust cybersecurity and data governance frameworks. Increasing reliance on interconnected systems exposes critical infrastructure to cyber risks that can disrupt essential services. Establishing cybersecurity protocols, encryption standards, and incident response plans protects data and operational integrity. Data privacy regulations must safeguard personal and proprietary information while enabling legitimate data sharing for public benefit. Governance frameworks should define clear responsibilities for data management, ensuring accountability and ethical use of technology.

Equitable access to digital technologies remains a challenge, particularly in low-income and rural regions. The digital divide limits the capacity of some communities to benefit from advanced monitoring and management systems. Expanding digital infrastructure, including broadband connectivity and sensor networks, supports inclusivity and resilience. Capacity building is essential to equip institutions, farmers, and local communities with the skills needed to use digital tools effectively. Partnerships among governments, private sectors, and development organizations can accelerate technology transfer and foster innovation tailored to local contexts.

The environmental footprint of digital technologies must also be managed. Data centers, electronic devices, and communication networks require energy and materials that contribute to emissions and waste. Transitioning to renewable-powered data infrastructure and promoting circular economy principles in technology production mitigate these impacts. Designing energy-efficient systems and extending product lifecycles contribute to sustainable digitalization.

Integrating AI, IoT, and remote sensing into Nexus governance provides opportunities to enhance efficiency, transparency, and resilience. Digital systems enable real-time responses to resource challenges and support long-term strategic planning through continuous learning and adaptation. As technology evolves, ensuring equitable access, data integrity, and environmental responsibility will be essential for realizing the full potential of digitalization in sustainable resource management.

Circular Economy Technologies

Circular economy technologies provide mechanisms for reducing waste, conserving resources, and improving efficiency across interconnected systems. Within the WEFEC Nexus, circularity focuses on closing resource loops to ensure that outputs from one process serve as inputs for another. Technological innovation in recycling, recovery, and reuse supports sustainable development by minimizing dependence on finite resources and reducing environmental pressures.

Water recycling and reuse technologies are central to circular economy applications. Advanced treatment processes such as membrane filtration, reverse osmosis, and ultraviolet disinfection enable safe recovery of wastewater for non-potable and, in some cases, potable uses. Urban water recycling systems reclaim greywater from domestic and industrial sources for irrigation, cooling, or industrial processes. In agriculture, treated wastewater supports irrigation in water-scarce regions, reducing pressure on freshwater resources. Decentralized water reuse systems integrated into urban infrastructure promote local resilience by reducing reliance on centralized supply networks.

Nutrient recovery technologies transform waste streams into valuable resources for agriculture and industry. Processes such as anaerobic digestion, struvite precipitation, and composting recover nitrogen, phosphorus, and organic matter from wastewater, manure, and food waste. Recovered nutrients are converted into biofertilizers or soil amendments, reducing dependency on synthetic fertilizers derived from fossil fuels. This closed-loop approach not only enhances soil health but also mitigates nutrient pollution in aquatic systems. Innovations in biorefineries expand nutrient recovery by integrating waste-to-energy and waste-to-material pathways, creating multifunctional resource recovery hubs.

Energy recovery technologies harness residual energy from waste streams, improving overall system efficiency. Anaerobic digestion of organic waste generates biogas, which can be used for electricity, heating, or as a renewable transport fuel. Wastewater treatment plants increasingly incorporate combined heat and power systems to capture energy from sludge digestion, achieving partial or full energy self-sufficiency. Industrial symbiosis initiatives promote heat recovery from manufacturing processes, supplying nearby facilities or district heating networks. These systems reduce greenhouse gas emissions and optimize energy use across sectors.

Technologies supporting material recycling close the loop on solid waste management. Mechanical and chemical recycling convert plastic, metal, and organic waste into secondary raw materials. Innovations in sorting, separation, and reprocessing technologies increase the quality and market value of recycled materials. Bio-based materials and biodegradable packaging reduce reliance on non-renewable inputs while minimizing waste generation. Circular manufacturing systems integrate life-cycle design principles to extend product durability, facilitate repair, and enable component reuse. These approaches reduce material throughput and environmental impacts while fostering industrial innovation.

Digital technologies enhance circular economy operations by enabling monitoring, optimization, and transparency. The IoT supports real-time tracking of resource flows, waste generation, and system performance. Smart sensors in water and energy networks monitor consumption and detect inefficiencies, enabling predictive maintenance and adaptive control. AI and data analytics improve process optimization in recycling and treatment facilities, identifying opportunities for increased efficiency. Blockchain technology facilitates traceability across supply chains, ensuring accountability in waste management and resource recovery. Integrating digital solutions enhances coordination and operational control within circular systems.

Agricultural technologies that incorporate circular principles strengthen the sustainability of food systems. Precision farming techniques optimize water, fertilizer, and energy use through data-driven management. Controlled-environment agriculture, including hydroponics and aquaponics, recycles water and nutrients within closed systems, reducing waste and emissions. Livestock and crop systems can be integrated to recycle organic waste into feed or fertilizer, enhancing resource efficiency at the farm level. These technologies align food production with environmental stewardship and long-term resource sustainability.

Industrial ecology provides the framework for scaling circular economy technologies across regions. In eco-industrial parks, businesses exchange waste materials, energy, and by-products to create mutually beneficial resource loops. For example, excess heat from one facility can be used in another's production process, while wastewater from one operation can be treated and reused in a neighboring plant. This coordinated approach transforms waste into resources, reducing costs and environmental footprints. Policy incentives, regulatory frameworks, and financing mechanisms support the adoption of industrial symbiosis models by encouraging collaboration and investment in shared infrastructure.

Emerging innovations such as carbon capture, utilization, and storage (CCUS) further expand the potential of circular economy technologies. Captured carbon dioxide can be used in industrial processes, agriculture, and the production of synthetic fuels or building materials. Integration of CCUS with renewable energy systems enhances decarbonization while creating new value chains. Bioenergy with carbon capture and storage (BECCS) combines energy recovery with emissions reduction, linking circular and climate mitigation strategies.

Scaling up circular economy technologies requires alignment of infrastructure, governance, and market incentives. Policy frameworks that encourage innovation, standardization, and investment accelerate technology deployment. Public-private partnerships and knowledge-sharing platforms promote collaboration across sectors. Education and capacity building ensure that stakeholders understand and apply circular principles effectively.

Embedding circularity into the WEFEC Nexus creates systems that are regenerative, resource-efficient, and resilient to future challenges.

Renewable and Low-Carbon Innovations

Renewable and low-carbon innovations enable the transition toward integrated resource systems that align with climate and sustainability goals. Advances in clean energy generation, efficient desalination, and carbon capture technologies reduce greenhouse gas emissions while supporting water, food, and ecosystem security. The adoption of these technologies reflects the growing interdependence between energy systems, water resources, and environmental resilience.

Solar, wind, and geothermal energy technologies are central to the low-carbon transition. Solar photovoltaic (PV) systems have become more efficient and affordable, allowing widespread deployment across residential, industrial, and agricultural applications. Solar-powered irrigation systems reduce reliance on fossil fuels, improving water access in rural areas. Concentrated solar power (CSP) technologies integrate thermal energy storage, providing reliable electricity even during non-sunlight hours. Wind power, both onshore and offshore, continues to expand as a cost-competitive renewable source that complements solar variability. Geothermal energy provides a stable supply of heat and electricity, particularly in regions with favorable geological conditions, contributing to diversified and resilient energy portfolios.

Hydropower remains a key renewable source within the energy mix, offering dual benefits for power generation and water management. Run-of-river and small-scale hydropower systems minimize ecological disruption compared to large dams, supporting decentralized energy access. Integrating hydropower with other renewables enhances grid stability and flexibility. Pumped-storage hydropower provides large-scale energy storage by using excess electricity to move water uphill, releasing it later to generate power during peak demand. These technologies bridge the temporal gap between energy supply and consumption, strengthening overall system efficiency.

Efficient desalination technologies contribute to water security while reducing environmental impacts. Traditional thermal desalination methods are energy-intensive, but innovations in membrane-based systems such as reverse osmosis (RO), forward osmosis, and membrane distillation have improved energy efficiency and reduced costs. Coupling desalination plants with renewable energy sources, including solar and wind, eliminates dependence on fossil fuels and reduces emissions. Hybrid systems that integrate desalination with wastewater recycling or brine management technologies minimize waste discharge and enhance circularity within the water sector. Energy recovery devices incorporated into desalination operations further reduce energy consumption, making large-scale water supply more sustainable.

CCUS technologies mitigate emissions from both industrial and natural sources. Capture techniques include post-combustion, pre-combustion, and direct air capture methods that separate carbon dioxide from gas streams. The captured carbon can be stored in geological formations or reused in industrial processes such as enhanced oil recovery, concrete production, or synthetic fuel generation. Emerging carbon utilization technologies convert captured CO_2 into valuable products, including building materials and bio-based chemicals, creating new circular economy opportunities. Integration of CCUS with bioenergy systems, known as BECCS, offers the potential for negative emissions by removing carbon dioxide from the atmosphere while producing renewable energy.

Hydrogen technologies are increasingly recognized as a cornerstone of low-carbon transitions. Green hydrogen, produced through water electrolysis powered by renewable energy, offers a clean alternative for sectors that are difficult to decarbonize, such as heavy industry and transport. Hydrogen storage and distribution systems enable energy flexibility, linking electricity, heating, and mobility networks. Coupling hydrogen production with desalination and wastewater treatment systems creates synergies between energy and water sectors, optimizing resource use and supporting integrated Nexus solutions.

Bioenergy technologies also contribute to low-carbon innovation by transforming organic waste and biomass into energy. Anaerobic digestion, gasification, and pyrolysis convert agricultural residues, municipal waste, and forestry by-products into biogas, bio-oil, or biochar. These processes generate renewable energy while recovering nutrients and reducing waste volumes. Advanced biofuels derived from non-food feedstocks offer sustainable alternatives to conventional fuels, reducing competition with food production. Integrating bioenergy systems with carbon capture enhances emission reductions and contributes to climate mitigation targets.

Grid modernization and energy storage technologies complement renewable deployment by improving flexibility and reliability. Battery storage systems, including lithium-ion and emerging solid-state designs, balance supply and demand fluctuations associated with variable renewables. Smart grids enable two-way communication between producers and consumers, optimizing energy distribution and minimizing losses. Integrating renewable microgrids with digital control systems enhances resilience in remote or disaster-prone regions by ensuring continuous energy access independent of centralized networks.

Innovations in building and industrial efficiency further support low-carbon transitions. Energy-efficient materials, green building designs, and waste heat recovery technologies reduce demand across sectors. Electrification of heating, cooling, and transport powered by renewables accelerates the decarbonization of end-use systems. Industrial symbiosis, where waste heat or by-products from one facility serve as inputs for another, maximizes energy efficiency within production networks. These strategies link energy, water, and material efficiency, reinforcing Nexus coherence across urban and industrial systems.

Renewable and low-carbon technologies contribute not only to emission reduction but also to resource diversification and resilience. Integrating these innovations into water, food, and energy planning supports sustainable growth while safeguarding ecosystem integrity. As technology advances and costs decline, coordinated policy, investment, and governance frameworks are necessary to accelerate deployment and ensure equitable access across regions and sectors.

Knowledge Sharing and Capacity Development

Knowledge sharing and capacity development are essential components of effective implementation of the WEFEC Nexus. Building institutional, technical, and social capacities enables countries and communities to adopt integrated approaches that promote sustainability, resilience, and innovation. Education, open data access, and professional training foster collaboration and ensure that knowledge and technologies are equitably distributed across sectors and regions.

Education establishes the foundation for Nexus understanding and application. Integrating Nexus concepts into curricula at all levels— from primary education to advanced university programs—develops a generation of professionals equipped to address interconnected resource challenges. Multidisciplinary programs in environmental management, engineering, and policy help students connect theoretical knowledge with practical applications. Vocational training and technical education also play a role in preparing the workforce for careers in renewable energy, sustainable agriculture, and ecosystem management. Educational institutions serve as knowledge hubs where research, innovation, and policy converge, supporting long-term capacity building.

Open data platforms enhance transparency and accessibility of information critical for Nexus planning. Data sharing among government agencies, research institutions, and private sectors enables integrated analysis of water, energy, land, and climate systems. Open access to datasets on resource flows, infrastructure, and environmental indicators supports evidence-based decision-making and collaborative governance. International initiatives that standardize data collection and reporting practices promote comparability and consistency across borders. Digital repositories and cloud-based platforms allow stakeholders to access, analyze, and visualize information, bridging gaps between knowledge producers and users.

Research and innovation networks facilitate the generation and exchange of knowledge relevant to the Nexus. Collaborative research programs that connect universities, think tanks, and policy institutions promote interdisciplinary approaches to resource management. Joint studies on system interdependencies and emerging technologies provide insights into sustainable solutions. Regional knowledge-sharing initiatives enable countries facing similar challenges to exchange best practices, develop joint projects, and strengthen institutional cooperation. International partnerships supported by organizations and development agencies help transfer research findings into actionable policy recommendations.

Professional training programs enhance the technical capabilities of practitioners working across water, energy, food, and environmental sectors. Workshops, certification programs, and online courses provide up-to-date knowledge on Nexus-related tools and methods. Training modules focused on integrated resource assessment, modeling, and governance equip policymakers and planners with the skills required for cross-sectoral coordination. Tailored programs for local communities and small enterprises ensure that capacity building extends beyond formal institutions, empowering stakeholders to participate actively in sustainable resource management.

Knowledge-sharing platforms, including conferences, webinars, and digital communities of practice, promote dialogue and collaboration among diverse actors. These forums facilitate the dissemination of new research, policy innovations, and technological advancements. They also create opportunities for networking and joint problem-solving across geographical and institutional boundaries. Online platforms supported by interactive tools such as dashboards and discussion forums enhance the reach and inclusivity of capacity development efforts.

South–South and triangular cooperation initiatives strengthen capacity development by fostering peer-to-peer learning among developing countries. Through knowledge exchange, technical missions, and joint training programs, countries share context-specific experiences in implementing integrated resource management. These collaborations help build institutional resilience and reduce dependence on external expertise. Linking national efforts to regional centers of excellence enhances the sustainability of capacity-building outcomes.

Institutional strengthening supports the translation of knowledge into practice. Establishing dedicated Nexus units within ministries or inter-agency platforms enhances coordination and policy coherence. Embedding capacity development in national planning processes ensures that skills and knowledge are systematically updated to reflect evolving priorities. Partnerships between government institutions, academia, and the private sector promote applied research and the practical implementation of integrated solutions. Ensuring long-term institutional support through financing and policy commitments maintains momentum for continuous learning.

Gender equality and social inclusion are integral to effective capacity development. Women, Indigenous peoples, and marginalized communities often possess local knowledge critical to sustainable resource management but are underrepresented in decision-making. Inclusive education and training initiatives that recognize diverse knowledge systems enhance social equity and innovation. Programs that empower women and youth with technical and leadership skills expand participation in Nexus-related sectors and promote equitable benefits from technological advancement.

Monitoring and evaluation systems assess the effectiveness of knowledge-sharing and capacity-development initiatives. Indicators tracking participation rates, knowledge transfer outcomes, and institutional performance provide feedback for improving program design. Periodic evaluations identify strengths, gaps, and opportunities for scaling successful practices. Continuous learning ensures that capacity development remains adaptive to technological advances, policy shifts, and environmental change.

Effective knowledge sharing and capacity development depend on collaboration, transparency, and inclusivity. By investing in education, open data, and training, societies can strengthen institutional resilience and enable equitable access to innovations that support sustainable management of interconnected resource systems.

Chapter 9: Financing and Implementation Pathways

Financing and implementation pathways determine how effectively the WEFEC Nexus can be realized in practice. Achieving integrated sustainability goals requires mobilizing diverse funding sources, including public investment, private capital, and international climate finance. Aligning these financial flows with Nexus objectives ensures that resource-efficient projects receive long-term support. Green bonds, blended finance, and performance-based instruments enable cost-sharing and risk mitigation across sectors. Implementation depends on coherent institutional frameworks, transparent monitoring, and capacity-building initiatives. When financial mechanisms are strategically designed to promote collaboration and innovation, they accelerate the transition toward sustainable and resilient resource systems worldwide.

Investment Needs and Financial Mechanisms

Achieving the objectives of the WEFEC Nexus requires significant investment in infrastructure, innovation, and institutional capacity. Mobilizing financial resources to support integrated, cross-sectoral projects is critical for advancing sustainable development and climate resilience. Diverse financing mechanisms—including green bonds, climate funds, and blended finance instruments—play essential roles in aligning capital flows with Nexus priorities and ensuring that investment decisions reflect long-term social, economic, and environmental benefits.

Investment needs across the Nexus are substantial due to growing demands for clean energy, efficient water systems, sustainable agriculture, and ecosystem restoration. Infrastructure in many regions requires modernization to cope with climate variability and resource scarcity. Water treatment facilities, irrigation networks, renewable energy systems, and resilient food production chains all depend on coordinated financing approaches. Public budgets alone are insufficient to address these challenges, highlighting the importance of private sector participation and international financial cooperation. Mobilizing investment at scale requires clear policy signals, supportive regulatory frameworks, and mechanisms that reduce risk for investors.

Green bonds have emerged as a major instrument for financing environmentally sustainable projects. These fixed-income securities channel capital into initiatives that generate measurable environmental benefits, such as renewable energy, wastewater treatment, sustainable agriculture, and ecosystem rehabilitation. Green bond frameworks provide transparency through the use of proceeds reporting and third-party verification. Governments, municipalities, and corporations increasingly issue green bonds to fund Nexus-related investments that contribute to climate mitigation and adaptation. The expansion of green bond markets promotes investor confidence and diversifies funding sources for integrated resource projects.

Climate funds complement private and public investment by providing concessional financing for projects aligned with global climate objectives. Multilateral mechanisms such as the GCF, GEF, and Adaptation Fund support developing countries in implementing Nexus-oriented strategies. These funds often prioritize initiatives that deliver multiple co-benefits across water, energy, agriculture, and ecosystem management. By offering grants, low-interest loans, and technical assistance, climate funds reduce financial barriers and enable the scaling of innovative solutions. National climate finance strategies enhance access to these resources by aligning domestic priorities with international funding criteria.

Blended finance mechanisms leverage public capital to attract private investment in sustainable infrastructure. By combining concessional and commercial finance, blended models reduce project risk and improve returns for investors. Instruments such as guarantees, first-loss capital, and results-based payments make cross-sectoral projects more bankable. For example, a blended finance approach can support renewable-powered desalination plants, integrating energy and water objectives within a single investment framework. Development finance institutions (DFIs) and multilateral development banks (MDBs) play central roles in structuring such arrangements, facilitating collaboration between governments, investors, and technology providers.

Private sector investment is increasingly vital to advancing Nexus goals. Companies in energy, water, and agriculture sectors recognize the business case for sustainable practices that improve efficiency and reduce exposure to resource risks. Impact investors and sustainability-focused funds channel capital into projects that generate both financial returns and positive environmental outcomes. Corporate sustainability bonds and sustainability-linked loans tie financing terms to performance indicators such as emissions reduction, water conservation, or renewable energy integration. Encouraging private investment in Nexus projects requires stable policy environments, clear standards, and incentives for long-term engagement.

Public finance remains essential for building enabling conditions and supporting projects that may not attract private capital. Government expenditures on research, education, and infrastructure lay the groundwork for sustainable transitions. Public investment in early-stage technologies helps bridge the gap between innovation and commercialization. Policy tools such as tax incentives, feed-in tariffs, and water pricing reforms can stimulate private sector participation while promoting efficiency. Fiscal instruments aligned with environmental objectives ensure that public funds contribute to the broader sustainability agenda.

International cooperation enhances financial flows for Nexus implementation, particularly in developing and climate-vulnerable countries. Development partners and multilateral institutions provide funding, risk-sharing instruments, and technical support to strengthen national capacities for project design and financial management. Cross-border investments in regional infrastructure, such as transboundary water management or energy interconnections, promote shared benefits and reduce collective risks. Coordinated financial planning among neighboring countries encourages resource-sharing arrangements and joint access to international climate finance.

Innovative financial instruments are expanding the range of options available for Nexus investments. Sustainability-linked derivatives, outcome-based financing, and environmental impact bonds tie financial returns to measurable sustainability outcomes. PES schemes compensate landowners and communities for maintaining forests, wetlands, and watersheds that deliver water regulation, carbon sequestration, and biodiversity benefits. Insurance-linked instruments such as climate resilience bonds provide coverage against climate-related losses, protecting investments in critical infrastructure and livelihoods. The integration of these instruments into financial systems enhances flexibility and supports adaptive management.

Transparent and standardized metrics are essential for evaluating the environmental and social performance of Nexus investments. Taxonomies and disclosure frameworks, such as those developed under the European Union's Sustainable Finance initiative, guide investors toward sustainable assets. Monitoring and reporting mechanisms ensure accountability and facilitate assessment of long-term impacts. Integrating sustainability indicators into credit assessments and investment risk models enables financial institutions to align portfolios with climate and resource objectives.

Capacity development in financial governance supports the effective implementation of Nexus-aligned financing strategies. Governments and financial institutions require expertise in project appraisal, risk management, and cross-sectoral coordination. Establishing dedicated green finance units within ministries or banks improves oversight and integration of environmental considerations into investment planning. Collaboration between finance ministries, central banks, and development partners enhances policy coherence and resource mobilization.

Achieving Nexus objectives depends on aligning financial systems with sustainability goals. Mobilizing capital through a combination of green bonds, climate funds, blended finance, and innovative instruments ensures that investments generate lasting economic, environmental, and social value. A coordinated financial architecture supports the transformation toward resource-efficient, climate-resilient, and inclusive development pathways.

Public–Private Partnerships and Market Instruments

Public–private partnerships (PPPs) and market-based instruments provide mechanisms for mobilizing capital, technology, and expertise to achieve integrated resource management within the WEFEC Nexus. These approaches combine the efficiency and innovation capacity of the private sector with the oversight and public-interest orientation of governments. When designed effectively, they facilitate the development of sustainable infrastructure, promote innovation, and enhance resource-use efficiency while maintaining accountability and environmental protection.

PPPs enable collaboration between public authorities and private entities in financing, building, and operating infrastructure and services. Governments typically retain ownership or regulatory control, while private partners contribute technical knowledge, financial resources, and operational capabilities. In water management, PPPs can support wastewater treatment, desalination, and irrigation infrastructure. In the energy sector, they are used for renewable energy generation, smart grids, and energy-efficient technologies. Agricultural PPPs promote innovation in supply chains, sustainable farming practices, and value addition. Structuring PPPs within the Nexus framework ensures that projects consider interdependencies across sectors rather than focusing on isolated outcomes.

Successful PPPs require transparent legal and regulatory frameworks that define the rights, obligations, and responsibilities of all parties.

Clear contractual arrangements establish performance standards, risk-sharing mechanisms, and accountability measures. Governments play a critical role in setting sustainability criteria, environmental standards, and social safeguards to guide private investment toward Nexus-aligned objectives. Effective regulation ensures that private participation does not compromise public service quality or accessibility. Independent oversight bodies and grievance mechanisms help maintain public trust and accountability throughout project implementation.

Risk allocation is central to PPP design. Public and private partners must balance commercial viability with public benefit. Risks associated with construction, financing, and operation are often transferred to the private sector, while governments retain policy, regulatory, and social responsibilities. Instruments such as viability gap funding and partial risk guarantees help bridge financial feasibility gaps for projects that deliver high social or environmental value but limited immediate returns. Careful assessment of financial and environmental risks supports the long-term sustainability of PPP arrangements.

Market-based instruments complement PPPs by using economic incentives to encourage efficient resource use and environmental stewardship. Pricing mechanisms, taxes, and tradable permits internalize environmental costs and align market behavior with sustainability goals. For example, water pricing policies that reflect scarcity values encourage conservation and efficient allocation. Energy pricing reforms eliminate subsidies that promote overconsumption and create incentives for renewable energy adoption. Carbon pricing mechanisms, including emissions trading systems and carbon taxes, drive investment toward low-carbon technologies and resource-efficient production.

Payments for ecosystem services (PES) represent a form of market instrument that rewards individuals, communities, or organizations for maintaining or restoring ecosystems that provide valuable services. These programs compensate landowners for actions such as reforestation, wetland conservation, or sustainable agriculture, which enhance water quality, biodiversity, and carbon sequestration. By assigning economic value to ecosystem services, PES programs bridge the gap between environmental protection and economic development. Governments, corporations, and international donors can collaborate to establish funding mechanisms that sustain these initiatives over the long term.

Green certification and labeling schemes serve as additional market instruments that influence consumer and corporate behavior. Certification programs verify compliance with environmental or social standards, creating incentives for producers to adopt sustainable practices. Labels such as those for organic agriculture, sustainable forestry, or renewable energy products inform consumers and drive demand for environmentally responsible goods. Market recognition for sustainability enhances brand reputation and competitiveness while contributing to broader environmental objectives.

Capital markets play an expanding role in financing Nexus-oriented projects through instruments such as green, blue, and sustainability-linked bonds. These securities provide investors with opportunities to fund projects that generate measurable environmental benefits. Corporate sustainability-linked loans tie interest rates to environmental performance indicators, motivating continuous improvement. Access to capital markets through such instruments diversifies funding sources and enables large-scale investment in integrated infrastructure projects.

Technology innovation and knowledge transfer are facilitated through PPPs that combine research capacity and practical application. Joint ventures between public research institutions and private firms accelerate the development of water-efficient technologies, renewable energy systems, and sustainable agricultural methods. Shared intellectual property frameworks ensure equitable distribution of benefits while promoting innovation diffusion. Collaborative innovation platforms supported by PPPs can foster start-up ecosystems focused on circular economy solutions and climate-resilient technologies.

Ensuring that PPPs and market instruments deliver public value requires strong governance and monitoring systems. Independent evaluation frameworks assess financial performance, social outcomes, and environmental impacts. Data transparency allows stakeholders to track progress and identify areas for improvement. Public disclosure of project terms, performance reports, and environmental assessments enhances accountability and confidence in private sector engagement. Institutional capacity building within government agencies ensures effective oversight and alignment of private initiatives with national sustainability goals.

Integrating PPPs and market instruments within the Nexus approach enables resource management that is both economically viable and environmentally sustainable. These mechanisms expand the range of financing and implementation options available to governments while engaging the private sector as an active partner in achieving long-term resilience and sustainability objectives.

International Cooperation and Development Aid

International cooperation and development aid play a central role in advancing the WEFEC Nexus by facilitating cross-border collaboration, financing sustainable infrastructure, and building institutional capacity. Multilateral and bilateral partnerships enable countries to share knowledge, align policies, and mobilize resources toward integrated solutions that address interlinked environmental and developmental challenges.

Multilateral institutions such as the World Bank, regional development banks, and United Nations agencies serve as key enablers of Nexus-related initiatives. They provide technical assistance, concessional financing, and policy support to help countries integrate water, energy, and food security into national development strategies. Through instruments like loans, grants, and blended finance, these institutions fund large-scale projects that deliver multiple co-benefits. The World Bank's investment programs in renewable energy and sustainable agriculture, for example, often include components addressing water conservation and ecosystem management. Regional development banks, including the African Development Bank and Asian Development Bank, prioritize cross-sectoral resilience-building projects aligned with climate adaptation and mitigation goals.

Bilateral aid agencies also contribute to Nexus implementation by supporting targeted interventions and capacity-building efforts. Development cooperation programs led by donor governments fund policy reforms, research partnerships, and pilot projects that demonstrate integrated resource management approaches. Agencies such as the German Agency for International Cooperation (GIZ), Japan International Cooperation Agency (JICA), and the United States Agency for International Development (USAID) promote Nexus-aligned initiatives through technical assistance, policy dialogue, and technology transfer. Bilateral support often complements multilateral financing by addressing country-specific needs, strengthening local governance systems, and fostering innovation.

Global climate and environmental funds provide additional resources for Nexus-aligned investments. Mechanisms such as the GCF, GEF, and Adaptation Fund finance initiatives that link climate resilience with sustainable resource management. These funds prioritize projects that generate multiple benefits, such as improving water efficiency, promoting renewable energy, and restoring ecosystems. Access to such funding requires strong institutional capacity and alignment with national climate commitments under the Paris Agreement. International cooperation helps countries develop project proposals that meet fund eligibility criteria and implement effective monitoring systems to ensure accountability.

Cross-border cooperation frameworks are essential for managing transboundary resources and regional ecosystems. Shared river basins, aquifers, and energy grids demand coordinated governance among neighboring states. Multilateral organizations facilitate dialogue and joint planning to prevent conflict and promote equitable resource sharing. River basin commissions and regional agreements establish mechanisms for data exchange, joint infrastructure development, and climate adaptation planning. International organizations such as the FAO and the United Nations Economic Commission for Europe (UNECE) support the harmonization of legal and institutional frameworks for transboundary cooperation.

Capacity building and technical assistance programs strengthen institutions and human resources in developing countries, ensuring that international investments achieve long-term impact. Training initiatives in integrated resource management, data analysis, and policy coordination enhance the ability of governments to design and implement Nexus-informed strategies. Development partners often establish regional knowledge platforms that foster learning among countries facing similar challenges. These platforms disseminate best practices, facilitate peer-to-peer exchanges, and encourage collaboration between public agencies, research institutions, and civil society.

Technology transfer is a critical component of international cooperation, enabling the adoption of innovative solutions that improve resource efficiency and reduce emissions. Multilateral and bilateral programs support the dissemination of renewable energy technologies, smart irrigation systems, and digital monitoring tools. Partnerships between research institutions and private enterprises help adapt technologies to local contexts. Technical cooperation agreements ensure that recipient countries not only receive technology but also build the skills and infrastructure necessary for long-term application and maintenance.

Development aid also supports policy and regulatory reforms that create enabling environments for Nexus investments. Donor-funded programs assist governments in updating legislation, establishing resource pricing systems, and integrating environmental standards into national policies. Policy coherence across water, energy, and agricultural sectors enhances investment effectiveness and ensures alignment with international commitments such as the SDGs. Policy-based lending instruments offered by multilateral banks provide financial incentives for reforms that strengthen cross-sectoral governance and resource management.

Monitoring and evaluation mechanisms ensure that international aid contributes to measurable outcomes. Donors and recipients jointly develop performance indicators that track progress in achieving water access, energy efficiency, food security, and ecosystem restoration targets. Transparent reporting enhances accountability and encourages continuous learning. Data sharing between institutions and countries improves coordination and helps align aid with national priorities and regional strategies.

Emerging forms of cooperation, including South–South and triangular partnerships, expand the scope of international collaboration. These models promote knowledge exchange and technology transfer among developing countries, leveraging shared experiences and regional expertise. By fostering mutual learning and co-financing arrangements, they complement traditional aid mechanisms and strengthen collective capacity to address global sustainability challenges.

International cooperation and development aid create the financial and institutional foundations for implementing Nexus-based approaches. By integrating technical assistance, policy reform, and infrastructure investment, multilateral and bilateral partners help countries achieve balanced, resource-efficient, and climate-resilient development outcomes.

Measuring Success and Long-Term Impacts

Monitoring frameworks provide structured approaches to assess progress toward achieving objectives within the WEFEC Nexus. These frameworks help track performance, identify gaps, and guide adaptive management across interconnected systems. Establishing clear indicators and data collection processes ensures that resource management and policy implementation are aligned with sustainable outcomes.

Effective monitoring begins with defining measurable indicators that reflect Nexus objectives, such as water efficiency, renewable energy expansion, food productivity, and ecosystem health. Indicators should capture both quantitative and qualitative aspects of performance, including environmental, social, and economic dimensions. For example, energy intensity in water supply systems, agricultural water productivity, and biodiversity indices provide insights into cross-sectoral efficiency and resilience. Selecting appropriate indicators requires a balance between comprehensiveness and practicality, ensuring that data can be collected consistently and meaningfully interpreted.

Data collection and management systems form the foundation of monitoring frameworks. Integrating geospatial data, remote sensing, and ground-based observations enables continuous tracking of environmental conditions and resource use. Digital platforms that combine data from multiple sectors allow for real-time assessment of interdependencies across water, energy, food, and ecosystem systems. Ensuring data quality, interoperability, and accessibility is essential to support informed decision-making. Partnerships between government agencies, research institutions, and private organizations can enhance data coverage and reliability through coordinated monitoring networks.

Reporting and evaluation processes translate raw data into actionable insights. Periodic reporting on progress toward established targets promotes transparency and accountability among stakeholders. Evaluation frameworks assess the effectiveness of interventions and identify where adjustments are needed. For example, tracking the efficiency gains from water reuse technologies or the emission reductions achieved through renewable energy expansion provides evidence for scaling successful practices. Adaptive evaluation approaches ensure that policies remain responsive to emerging challenges and evolving priorities.

At the institutional level, integrating monitoring frameworks into national and regional planning supports coherence across sectors. Governments can embed performance indicators into budgetary and regulatory systems, linking resource allocation to measurable outcomes. Cross-ministerial committees and interagency platforms facilitate data sharing and coordinated evaluation. Aligning national monitoring efforts with international frameworks, such as the SDGs and the Paris Agreement, enhances comparability and fosters global accountability.

Socioeconomic and equity dimensions must also be incorporated into long-term monitoring. Evaluating the distributional effects of Nexus interventions helps ensure that benefits reach vulnerable populations and that policies promote inclusive development. Gender-sensitive and participatory monitoring approaches capture diverse perspectives and foster community ownership of outcomes. Including local stakeholders in data collection and assessment enhances the legitimacy of monitoring processes and strengthens adaptive capacity.

Scenario-based modeling and long-term forecasting complement traditional monitoring by anticipating future resource dynamics and policy impacts. Integrated assessment models simulate interactions between sectors under various climate and development pathways, informing strategic planning. These tools enable policymakers to evaluate how current actions influence long-term sustainability goals and to design adaptive strategies accordingly. Continuous refinement of models based on observed data enhances predictive accuracy and policy relevance.

Financial and institutional sustainability of monitoring frameworks is crucial for long-term impact. Establishing dedicated funding mechanisms ensures continuity in data collection, capacity building, and technological upgrades. Institutionalizing monitoring within existing governance structures reduces dependency on short-term projects and external funding cycles. Collaboration with international organizations can provide technical assistance and capacity support for maintaining comprehensive and enduring monitoring systems.

Evaluation of long-term impacts extends beyond immediate outcomes to consider cumulative and systemic effects. Understanding how Nexus interventions influence ecosystem resilience, economic productivity, and social stability over decades informs future policy and investment choices. Long-term impact assessments can reveal trade-offs or unintended consequences that short-term monitoring might overlook. Applying adaptive learning principles allows institutions to refine their strategies based on accumulated evidence and evolving environmental conditions.

The integration of robust monitoring and evaluation frameworks into Nexus governance ensures that progress is measurable, policies remain evidence-based, and systems evolve toward greater sustainability and resilience over time.

Conclusion

The WEFEC Nexus establishes an integrated framework for addressing the interconnections among natural and human systems. By viewing resource management through a systems-based perspective, societies can identify synergies and minimize conflicts that arise from competing sectoral demands. The Nexus approach enables policies and investments that enhance resilience, promote sustainability, and secure long-term development outcomes.

Integrated governance is central to operationalizing the Nexus. Institutions that traditionally manage water, energy, food, and environmental resources independently must coordinate policies and strategies. Such coordination ensures that the use of one resource does not undermine another. Embedding Nexus principles into planning frameworks helps align resource efficiency, social equity, and environmental protection within national and regional agendas.

Technology innovation plays a critical role in supporting Nexus integration. Advances in renewable energy, water reuse, precision agriculture, and ecosystem monitoring improve efficiency across interconnected systems. Digital tools, such as artificial intelligence and remote sensing, enable data-driven decision-making and enhance real-time management. Technology deployment must be accompanied by policies that encourage equitable access and knowledge sharing to ensure that all sectors and communities benefit from innovation.

Financing mechanisms determine the pace and scale of Nexus implementation. Mobilizing investment through green bonds, blended finance, and public–private partnerships supports projects that deliver multiple benefits across water, energy, food, and ecosystem systems. Aligning financial flows with sustainability criteria directs capital toward interventions that contribute to resilience and climate goals. International funding mechanisms, including climate and development finance, expand opportunities for collaborative action and capacity building.

Human and institutional capacity underpin the success of the Nexus approach. Education, training, and participatory governance strengthen local ownership and accountability. Integrating Nexus concepts into professional curricula and policy training programs builds a workforce capable of managing complex interdependencies. Open data platforms and collaborative research networks facilitate the exchange of knowledge and promote continuous learning across disciplines and regions.

The increasing intensity of climate impacts underscores the need for systemic approaches that transcend sectoral boundaries. Variability in rainfall, temperature extremes, and shifting ecosystem functions place additional strain on water, energy, and food systems. Adaptation and mitigation strategies designed within the Nexus framework can deliver cross-sectoral co-benefits, supporting both human development and environmental sustainability.

Policy coherence and international collaboration are essential for scaling Nexus-based solutions. Global commitments under frameworks such as the Sustainable Development Goals, the Paris Agreement, and the Convention on Biological Diversity provide opportunities to integrate Nexus thinking into shared objectives. Cooperation across borders ensures that transboundary resources are managed collectively and equitably, contributing to regional stability and global resilience.

The WEFEC Nexus offers a comprehensive approach to achieving sustainability in an era of uncertainty and resource constraints. By integrating governance, technology, finance, and capacity development, it provides a foundation for resilient societies capable of adapting to environmental change and advancing sustainable growth.

www.ingramcontent.com/pod-product-compliance
Lightning Source LLC
Chambersburg PA
CBHW071602200326
41519CB00021BB/6843